THE
NEW YORK
YANKEES

AN ILLUSTRATED HISTORY

THE
NEW YORK
YANKEES
AN ILLUSTRATED HISTORY

Mark Gallagher, Neil Gallagher and Jim Kaplan

JG PRESS

Published by World Publications Group, Inc.
140 Laurel Street
East Bridgewater, MA 02333
www.wrldpub.com

ISBN 1464300410
978-1-4643-0041-7

Printed and bound in China by Toppan Leefung
Printing Limited.

PICTURE CREDITS

The Bettmann Archive: 18, 21
Chris Faytok/Star-Ledger/Corbis: 94
David Bergman/Corbis: 95
Getty Images: 2, 78, 79, 80, 81, 82, 83, 98 (both),
    99, 100, 101 (both), 102 (both), 103 (bottom), 104
    (both), 105 (bottom), 106, 107 (both), 108, 109, 110,
111, 112, 113, 113 (both), 114, 115, 116, 117, 118
Jason Szenes/epa/Corbis: 97
Major League Baseball via Getty Images: 84, 103
    (top), 105 (top)
Malcolm Emmons: 52
Mike Segar/Reuters/Corbis: 96
Mitchell Layton/NewSport/Corbis: 90
Nancy Hogue: 49, 50 (top), 56, 60 (both)
National Baseball Library, Cooperstown, NY: 13,
    15 (both), 19, 26 (top), 28, 35, 39, 50 (bottom),
    54 (top)
Ponzini Photography: 3, 53, 55, 57, 61 (both), 62-63,
    65, 66 (top), 67 (top), 69, 70, 71 (top), 72 (both),
    73, 74 (both), 75, 76, 77 (all three)
Reuters/Corbis: 6, 85, 86, 87, 88, 89, 91, 92, 93
TOPPS Baseball Cards: 7 (all four)
UPI/Bettmann Newsphotos: 1, 4-5, 8 (both), 9, 10,
    11, 12 (both), 14, 16-17, 20, 22 (both), 23, 24, 25,
    26 (bottom), 27, 29 (both), 30, 31, 32 (both), 33,
    34, 36 (both), 37, 38, 40-41 (all three), 42, 43, 44,
    45 (both), 46, 47, 48, 51, 54 (bottom), 58-59, 64, 66
    (bottom), 67 (bottom), 68, 71 (bottom)
Endpaper photo courtesy of New York Yankees

ACKNOWLEDGMENTS

The author and publisher would like to thank the
following people who have helped in the preparation
of this book: Barbara Thrasher, Don Longabucco,
Rita Longabucco, Elizabeth McCarthy, Jack Tom,
Kevin Ullrich, John S. Bowman, and Doron "Duke"
Goldman for his contributions to the Achievements
and checking final chapters.

Page 1: *Joe Di Maggio, here in his rookie 1936 season, gets a hit against the Cleveland Indians. (Their catcher is Billy Sullivan.) In 1941, DiMaggio will hit in 56 consecutive games, a record many believe is unlikely ever to be broken.*

Page 2: *Derek Jeter in 2011 assured his place in the team's history not only with this 3,000th hit but by taking over first place with career games played and at bats.*

Page 3: *Mariano Rivera continued to be not just the dominant closer for the Yankees but in 2011 took over two all-time MLB records— saves (603) and games finished (883).*

This Page: *Babe Ruth stands in the midst of a portion of the 5,000 boys who had gathered to see the great Bambino in Syracuse, New York, in August 1922*

Contents

Preface

Ask tourists gazing awe-struck at skyscrapers what New York City landmarks they'd like to see. Chances are they'll say the Empire State Building, the Statue of Liberty, the Brooklyn Bridge, a few museums — and Yankee Stadium. Since 2009, they're going to be seeing the brand new stadium, but at least some of the old mystique has carried over along with the plaques honoring the all-time Yankee greats. And true fans will close their eyes and evoke some of the great moments in the old stadium's past: from Ruth's homer to open the place in 1923 to Reggie Jackson's three dingers on his only three swings in the '77 Series finale to the amusing pine-tar incident of 1983.

Now, thanks to their winning the World Series of 2009, the Yankee tradition of exciting baseball has been carried over to the new Yankee Stadium. For the fact is, that when queried about the most impressive sports teams of all time, many respondents will cite the New York Yankees. Their lordships have won 40 pennants and 27 World

Championships, a feat unrivalled in North American sports. And they've done it with such panache that boys from remote and distant corners of North — and even South-America are known to adopt the name "Yankees."

To be sure, many people don't like the Yankees. Growing up in New York City, Red Sox G.M. Theo Epstein was told by his father not to root for them. "They're bullies and bankers," the elder Epstein said. And he might have added bigots, at least in the past tense, because of the team's refusal to integrate until 1955. Others claim the Yankees win titles only because they outspend everyone else, an assertion belied by Yankee frustrations over the eight free-spending seasons prior to 2009. Some of the charges hold water; certainly the club's long-time owner, George Steinbrenner, tried to bully everyone from his employees to the mayor of New York City. On the other hand, much Yankee hatred comes from pure jealousy or resentment against a Gotham-based institution getting outsized coverage. To review Yankee

Below: *Derek Jeter, the dynamic Yankee captain and short-stop, completes a double play against the Angels.*

Opposite: *Four baseball cards depict Yankee stars from four eras.*

JOE DIMAGGIO
Outfield

YANKEES

WHITEY FORD
Pitcher

YANKEES

Topps

Yankees
DON MATTINGLY

ROGER MARIS
Outfield

YANKEES

Right: *Yankee manager Joe McCarthy (left) poses with his big guns — Babe Ruth and Lou Gehrig — at 1934 spring training in St. Petersburg, Florida. Although the Yanks would finish second to Detroit, Gehrig turned in a Triple Crown performance that year.*

Below: *Manager Casey Stengel (left center) leads the Yankees in a victory cheer after they defeated the Red Sox 5-3 on October 2, 1949, to take the pennant.*

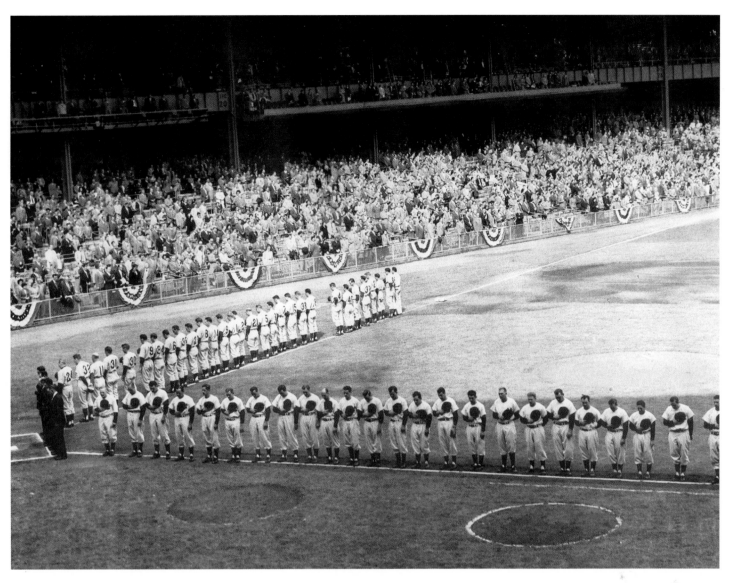

history, as we did in updating this book, is to find a much better case for the Yankees as a positive force in American society. Babe Ruth and his power stroke earn credit for helping to rescue the game when news broke of the Black Sox scandal in 1920. A wonderfully outrageous character, Ruth personified the Roaring Twenties. Casey Stengel's managing probably dwarfs that of any supervisor in any sport. The Yankees won 10 pennants and seven World Championships during his 12-year (1949-60) reign. And the Old Perfesser may have been the most quotable figure in sport. You could look it up.

The Yankees have provided some of the most inspiring stories that sport has brought to the larger stage. When Joe DiMaggio was establishing his record 56-game hitting streak in 1941, Americans happily turned from their worries about impending war to follow him on the radio or in the newspapers. *Baseball in '41* author Robert W. Creamer describes how his buddy Andy Crichton and three friends paused on a cross-country trip at a Montana eatery: "Almost every man who came into the café, Crichton said, would glance toward a newspaper lying on the counter and ask the proprietor, 'He get one yesterday?'"

DiMaggio was later immortalized in the Simon & Garfunkel song "Mrs. Robinson": "Where have you gone, Joe DiMaggio? / A nation turns its lonely eyes to you" (The song's lyricist, Paul Simon, confessed to being a bigger fan of another Yankee centerfielder, Mickey Mantle, but the syllables didn't fit the beat!) Twenty years after the Yankee Clipper's feat, a nation turned its eager eyes toward another Yankee, Roger Maris, who was chasing Ruth's single-season home-run record of 60. Purists scoffed that the two men didn't belong in the same sentence, and Maris suffered worry (and hair loss) during the ordeal. But after he hit #61 on the last day of the '61 season, the image of a kindler, gentler Maris began to emerge. Among other things Maris, who died of cancer in 1985 at age 51, was a quiet crusader against anti-Semitism.

The most recent Mr. Yankee has been Derek Jeter, a mixed-race shortstop. It might even be said that sterling sports stars like Jeter prepared Americans to accept a Barack Obama as president? In any case, the Yankee legend lives on in Jeter, and his teammates and will no doubt contribute to that legend in their new stadium.

JIM KAPLAN

Above: *The Yankees and their World Series opponents, the Phillies, observe a moment of silence for American soldiers in Korea before the start of game three in the 1950 Series. The New Yorkers swept the Phils to take their thirteenth World Championship.*

1. Becoming the Yankees

Babe Ruth led them from the shadow of John McGraw's New York Giants to the brightest sunshine of professional sports. And to lasting prominence as the New York Yankees.

Ten home runs was a lot when Ruth broke into the major leagues in 1914. In fact, Philadelphia's Frank "Home Run" Baker led the American League with eight that year. In Ruth's first year as a Yankee, 1920, he hit 54. From today's perspective 54 homers is believable. But in 1920 it must have seemed like 200 today. There wasn't a team in baseball in 1920 – a team – that hit 54 homers.

The young Ruth was more than a slugger. He was fast afoot and he was a fine defensive outfielder. His most prized record was the 29 and two-thirds straight scoreless innings he pitched in World Series competition in his early career with Boston. He was, moreover, "a parade all by himself," as one sportswriter put it. He was great baseball in colorful, personable wrappings, the most famous of America's famous for three decades.

Babe Ruth was the catch of Tillinghast L'Hommedieu Huston and Jacob Ruppert, who bought the Yankees in 1915, two years after the "Highlanders" nickname was chucked. "Til" Huston was an affable backslapper, a friend of Harry Frazee, the Boston Red Sox owner who let Huston know he might be induced to convert his Babe Ruth to cash. Ruppert and Huston seldom agreed, but they were united in wanting Ruth.

The day after Christmas, 1919 – the most important day in Yankee history – the Babe was dealt for $125,000 and other considerations. There never was a better buy. With Ruth the Yanks in 1920 drew 1,289,422 fans at home, then a major-league attendance record, and a gain of 670,258 over the previous year. The Babe, the Bambino, had taken the city by storm. On the sidewalks, in the coffee shops and bars – everywhere – New Yorkers wanted to know: "What'd the Bambino do today?"

After finishing a strong third in 1920, the Yankees won their first American League pennant in 1921. The big test was a four-game set with contending Cleveland in the last days of September. Ruth's two home runs led them to a final-game victory which, with two previous wins, added up to a comfortable two-and-a-half-game lead over the Indians.

They took on the Giants in the World

Opposite: *Babe Ruth, pausing before a 1924 game to autograph a baseball, displays the cherubic facial features that inspired his nickname even after 10 big-league seasons.*

Left: *Yankee Stadium opens its doors for the first time, April 18, 1923.*

Series with all games played at the Polo Grounds where the Yankees were tenants of the Giants. It was the "inside baseball" of Giants manager McGraw, which emphasized the hit and run, the double steal and the squeeze play, against the power baseball of the Yankees. Inside baseball won.

The Yankees of 1922, after barely beating out St. Louis in a season-long dogfight, again faced the hotshot Giants. And again they were whipped in a bitter Series, with the Bambino and teammate Bob Meusel invading the Giants' locker room after one game in search of a heckler. It was more than field combat that engaged these two organizations. Theirs was a market war, and the "Invaders" were outdrawing the Giants in their own ballpark by 350,000.

In this year of 1922, as legend has it, the Giants told the Yankees to find their own ballpark. Ruppert and Huston bought a dozen acres in the Bronx across the Harlem River from the Polo Grounds and built America's first triple-deck stadium, and it was, Ruppert was to say, "a mistake. Not mine, but the Giants'." Yankee Stadium, soon to become the most famous sports palace in America, opened on April 18, 1923, and the 25,000 fans who had to be turned away couldn't even follow the game on the radio since the broadcast industry had not begun to cover baseball. Fittingly, on this day, Babe Ruth hit the first home run in "The House That Ruth Built."

Again in 1923 the Yankees captured the pennant, breezing this time, and again they faced the Giants in the World Series. In this six-game Series the Yankees prevailed,

Above: *Powerful Lou Gehrig rips a hit in a Florida exhibition game against the Boston Braves, March 19, 1929. The 1929 season would not be one of his best – only 35 homers, 126 RBIs, and a .300 batting average: outstanding for most ballplayers, but not vintage Gehrig.*

Right: *Yankees owner Jacob Ruppert watches batting practice before a 1926 game. Ruppert dressed his charges with the stylishness that characterized his own attire.*

thanks largely to the slugging of Ruth, who hit .368, with three homers and a triple. The Giants' moundsmen shied away from Ruth, walking him eight times, even though McGraw asserted they had "to pitch to better hitters than Ruth in the National League."

The stylish Ruppert, having put his team in pinstripes and blue stockings, in 1923 returned them to the dark blue caps of an earlier time. Ruppert, who bought out Huston early in the year for $1.5 million, was a happy man: "I now have baseball's greatest park, baseball's greatest players and baseball's greatest team."

Jake Ruppert, born to a wealthy family of brewers, had even more going for him. He was successful, polished, and he enjoyed the finer things of life. He was a social and political figure who served four terms in Congress. And he did have baseball's greatest players. Besides Ruth, there was hot-hitting Bob Meusel, an outfielder with a storied right arm; the fleet Whitey Witt in center field; Wally Pipp, who had .300-plus seasons in 1922 and 1923, at first base; Aaron Ward, Everett Scott and Jumpin' Joe Dugan at second, short and third; and, at catcher, the solid-hitting Wally Schang. His pitchers included Bob Shawkey, Carl Mays, Waite Hoyt, Bullet Joe Bush, Sad

Sam Jones and, joining the club in 1923, Herb Pennock. The Red Sox supplied much of the pitching, and one other great baseball man besides Ruth, Edward Barrow. Disgusted with the Ruth transaction, Barrow moved from the Boston organization to

the Yankees' front office following the 1920 season. The bushy-browed, able and tough-in-every-way Barrow became the Yankees' successful general manager.

Ruth was red hot, collecting 59 homers and 171 RBIs in 1921 and scoring 177 runs, the latter a standing American League record. He drew what is still a major-league record 170 walks in 1923, a year in which he hit .393, his career high. His slugging averages of .847 in 1920 and .846 in 1921 are easily the highest ever. Ruth's 1922 numbers were down because he didn't get to play until late May. He had violated major-league rules by barnstorming after the 1921 season and was suspended, the first of several suspensions for various infractions in what proved a difficult year.

Also suspended was the Babe's fellow barnstormer and friend, Bob Meusel. The great outfielder and slugger was seemingly indifferent at times, with little to say to the press until late in has career, nudging sportswriter Frank Graham's line: "He's learning to say hello when it's time to say goodbye."

With the close of the great 1923 season, Ruppert had every right to be ecstatic. And how about that Gehrig kid? A homer, a triple, four doubles and five singles in 26 plate appearances! Ruppert's club was humming in every way possible. He alone made the executive decisions; he backed general manager Barrow, who made the business and personnel decisions; and Barrow backed manager Miller Huggins, who made the field decisions.

The club was far different from the team acquired just eight years earlier from William S. Devery and Frank J. Farrell, who had succeeded in planting an American League franchise in New York but had trouble nurturing it. The Yankees' roots extend beyond Farrell, Devery and the New York scene, however. They reach down the East Coast to Baltimore.

Baltimore in the 1890s had the Orioles of the National League and they were masters of inside baseball. They were vicious and tremendously successful, and they were led by their third baseman, John Joseph McGraw. They were broken up, however, and in 1899 Baltimore was one of four teams culled by the National League. In 1901 American League President Ban Johnson wanted to put a franchise in Baltimore, and he lured McGraw with an offer of stock in the club.

Johnson believed baseball was ready for two major leagues. When National League owners refused to discuss his ideas, he withdrew from the National Agreement that designated the National League as the game's only major league. His league was "major," too, Johnson ordained in 1901. The next two seasons were battle years, with Johnson making successful raids of National League stars and the Americans badly outdrawing the Nationals in 1902. Johnson was winning the war. His league was now entrenched in all the major cities except New York.

Johnson was also at war with his manager in Baltimore, McGraw. He clashed repeatedly with the umpire-baiting McGraw and finally suspended him indefinitely. McGraw, sensing he wasn't in Johnson's future plans, deserted Johnson, Baltimore and the American League before they deserted him, as he put it. He was lured to New York to manage the Giants, but not before he entered into a deal that gave John T. Brush, an old Johnson adversary, control over the Orioles. This was the same Brush who chaired the Executive Committee of a National League bent on war against the Americans! It was the same man who would sabotage the Baltimore club and then, late in 1902, buy controlling interest in the New York Giants, managed by the same John McGraw!

In the summer of 1902 Johnson revoked the Baltimore franchise for failing to field a team, and prepared to move it to New York. Besides being crucial to the American League's viability as a major league, the move to New York would offer an additional incentive – the opportunity to hit

Above: *The "Knight of Kennett Square," Herb Pennock, warming up. Pennock won 21 games for New York in 1924 and 23 in 1926.*

Above: *Aptly-named "Big Bill" Devery in a ceremonial moment. The co-owner of the early Yankees would run out of patience with both his team and his partner, Frank Farrell.*

deserters and future Hall of Famers, out-fielder Wee Willie Keeler and pitcher Happy Jack Chesbro. Keeler, the premier bat artist of his era – "I hit 'em where they ain't" – had a .376 lifetime batting average when he joined the club, but hit only .295 in seven Highlander seasons. Chesbro blossomed, setting standing American League records in 1904 of 41 wins (against 12 losses), 51 games started, and 48 complete games. But for a Chesbro wild pitch on the season's final day, New York might have won the 1904 pennant.

Another early New York standout was Hal Chase. The Californian, who cared little for the East and said as much, was a reliable hitter and one of the league's biggest draws as a defensive first baseman. But Chase, who was with New York from 1905 to 1913, was a tarnished star. A gambler, "Prince Hal" was suspected by at least two of his managers of throwing Yankee games, and was later linked to the Black Sox scandal.

New York twice finished second, but typically finished fifth or sixth, and twice ended up in last place in the pre-Ruth years.

The Giants had the use of Hilltop Park after a 1911 fire destroyed much of the Polo Grounds. In 1913 they, in turn, invited the Americans to share their restored facility on a rental basis, and the offer was accepted.

Devery and Farrell were increasingly fighting with their managers and with each other. They were anxious to unload the club and so they did, to Ruppert and Huston in 1915 for $460,000. The new owners may have had only three things in common: money, a season's box at the Polo Grounds, and a passion for the Giants. Now they were owners of the Yankees – it was like Chevrolet devotees buying into a Ford dealership. For Ruppert, it was not just a matter of having the wrong club; he saw himself saddled with "an orphan club."

Ruppert and Huston set out to build a winner. They obtained Wally Pipp from Detroit, then bought the contract of Bob Shawkey from the Philadelphia Athletics, and a little later that of the Athletics' Frank "Home Run" Baker. The Yankees finished fifth in 1915 and fourth in 1916, Shawkey going 23-14 the latter year and the Yankees leading the league in homers with 35. Pipp had 12 and Baker 10.

But everything came unglued in 1917. What hurt was the juxtaposition of the Yankees' sixth-place finish with the Giants' perch at the very top of the National League. McGraw and the Giants were New York's darlings. Ruppert went shopping for a replacement for manager Wild Bill Dono-

Brush and McGraw in their wallets. A raid-ending agreement in early 1903 acknowledged the American League as a major league and gave the Americans territorial rights in New York. About the same time, Johnson was introduced to Frank Farrell, a big-time gambler and owner of a racing stable, who, with his partner, "Big Bill" Devery, a retired police chief who was doing well in real estate, picked up the franchise for $18,000. The New York Highlanders were born.

The wheeler-dealer partners laughed at the Giant boast of using their political connections to have the city "run a street car over second base" of any planned ballpark. It was they who had the connections, and on a site in Washington Heights near a soon-to-open subway station (168th Street), they built modest American League Park, better known as Hilltop Park.

Johnson made sure the 1903 Highlanders had a big-name manager, Clark Griffith, and a first-rate roster. Among the early stars were a couple of National League van. Huston was not too busy with the war effort in Europe to inject his preference for Wilbert Robinson, but Ruppert followed the advice of Johnson and hired Miller Huggins, the uncharismatic skipper of the St. Louis Cardinals who had earned a law degree while playing baseball.

What turned out to be a great choice wasn't immediately apparent. The Yankees under Huggins finished in the first division in 1918, 1919 and 1920, but how could they not in 1920 with Ruth? The pennants in 1921 and 1922 were nice, but with expectations running high, the World Series losses to the Giants were hard to accept. Opinions on Huggins rose only after his team won the 1923 World Championship.

Following their three pennants and a World Championship, the Yankees seemed almost invincible, but the pinstripers were thwarted in their quest for a fourth straight flag, the 1924 pennant going to Washington. If 1924 was a year of denial, 1925 was a season of total disaster, the Yankees plummeting to seventh place.

Ruth the playboy was forever chewing, smoking, eating or drinking. The Babe in 1925 developed a stomach ailment – the "bellyache heard around the world," they called it – and hit only 25 homers in 98 games (leaving it to Meusel to lead the league in homers with 33). Huggins fined him $5,000 for insubordination, which seemed to get his attention. It was a bad year for Ruth and the Yankees but a good year for Huggins, who now was more in command.

At 5'6", the 135-pound Huggins was forced to look up to his brawny fun-seekers. His players, in turn, looked down on him, and not just literally; to them he was no great shakes as a manager. They were joined in this sentiment, in Hug's first years, by none other than Huston. So the

early going was rough on Huggins. But he enjoyed the solid support of Ruppert and Barrow and in time gained reasonable cooperation from his charges. He was a decent, up-front man who liked his players and remembered only the very worst acts of insubordination. While McGraw across the Harlem commanded, Little Hug appealed. Yet Huggins was to Waite Hoyt, that gentleman of baseball, who pitched for both

Below: *Skippers grace the 1921 Series program cover.*

Bottom: *Giant Heinie Groh triples in the first game of the 1922 Series at the Polo Grounds. Yankee Everett Scott takes the throw.*

HARRY M. STEVENS, PUBLISHER   PRICE 25 CENTS

GIANTS VS YANKEES

1921

JOHN McGRAW   MILLER HUGGINS

WORLDS CHAMPIONSHIP SERIES

POLO GROUNDS

managers, "the greatest manager who ever lived, barring none."

With the 1926 season the Yankees once again blossomed, claiming their fourth American League flag, just as Ruth, who hit .372 and led the league with 47 homers and 145 RBIs, had brazenly predicted. The Yankees had two players up from the minors, Tony Lazzeri at second base and Mark Koenig at shortstop, who were handling major-league pitching well. They, along with a quickly-maturing Lou Gehrig (107 RBIs) at first and Joe Dugan at third, made up an unexpectedly sound infield. The catching, if unspectacular, was solid, too.

With Ruth and Meusel in the outfield was the pleasant-faced Earle Combs who, in his third season, was established as one of the game's best lead-off men; this season he scored 113 runs. Pitchers Herb Pennock (23-11), Urban Shocker (19-11), and Hoyt (16-12) accounted for nearly two-thirds of the Yankee wins, all of which were needed. The 1926 season was a race, the fast-starting Yankees managing to hold on all the way to the World Series, where they were nipped by St. Louis.

The 1927 season was a runaway, the Yankees winning by 19 games. The Yankees had a .714 winning percentage with a record of 110-44. Many have called it, and many still call it, the greatest baseball team ever. There was the "Murderers' Row" of Ruth, Gehrig, Meusel, Lazzeri, Combs, Koenig and Dugan. Ruth, hitting 60 home runs, was challenged all season long by Gehrig, who hit 47 and collected a league-leading 175 RBIs. Meusel hit .337 and Lazzeri .309, each poking in more than 100 RBIs. Combs led the league in hits (231) and triples (23); and Koenig and Dugan hit .285 and .269, respectively. It was a formidable lineup.

Ruth's great single-season record owed to a spectacular September. He had four home runs in April, twelve in May, and nine each in June, July and August. In September he hit 17. His sixtieth, off Washington's Tom Zachary, was hit at Yankee Stadium on September 30.

Mated to the Yanks' explosive attack was an outstanding pitching staff led by Hoyt (22-7), the ERA champion at 2.63. Hoyt was a fine ballplayer but he was also a painter, singer and writer. "The Brooklyn Schoolboy" once noted that the secret of pitching "lies in getting a job with the Yankees." Behind Hoyt was gentlemanly Herb Pennock (19-8), one of the smartest pitchers of all time, then Shocker (18-6), Dutch Ruether (13-6), and George Pipgras (10-3). Wilcy Moore (19-7), discovered by Barrow in the low minors, led the league in saves

with 13 and became the Yankees' first great relief pitcher.

The team was solid defensively. Ruth was an excellent outfielder, Combs ran like a deer and Meusel had that rifle arm. Gehrig and Lazzeri were steady on the right side of the infield while Dugan and Koenig made big plays on the left side. A highly

Left: *The leading hitters of the famed "Murderers Row" were, from left: Earle Combs, Bob Meusel, Lou Gehrig and Babe Ruth. Some say the 1927 Yanks were the best baseball team ever. If so, Combs, Meusel, Gehrig and Ruth were the cream of the cream.*

competent catching corps was composed of Pat Collins, Johnny Grabowski and Benny Bengough.

The 1927 Yankees won the World Series in four games. It was over before it started, the Pittsburgh players watching in awe as the Yankees sent screaming drives to the outer reaches of vast Forbes Field in bat-ting practice. Still, it was the pitching of Pennock, Hoyt, Moore and Pipgras – hold-ing the Pirates to an average of two earned runs per game – that won it for New York. Was this team as good as the old Baltimore Orioles, ex-Oriole Wilbert Robinson was asked. "They would have beat our brains out," was Robinson's reply.

2. Winning was Their Habit

The ascendant Yankees were to become the entrenched Yankees, or, to some, the damn Yankees. In the dozen years from 1928 through 1939, they would enjoy a half-dozen pennants. They would become the jacket-and-tie elite of baseball. Life was good, but as the Yankees found at both ends of the dozen years, it wasn't permanent.

Popular pitcher Urban Shocker, 37, died of a heart ailment in 1928, and a year later Manager Miller Huggins was dead at 50. The Mighty Mite couldn't get a spur in his 1929 team and had other worries. His small appetite vanished and a sore developed under an eye. Coach Art Fletcher urged treatment but Hug declined: "Go to the doctor because I have a red spot on my face? Me, who took the spikes of Frank Chase and Fred Clarke?" On September 25, 1929, Huggins was dead from a form of blood poisoning. Among the Yankees to break down and cry was Babe Ruth, who was so often at odds with him.

Huggins had come to New York with nearly everyone against him. The funeral that took him away, with Ruth, Gehrig and other Yankees serving as pallbearers, touched all New Yorkers. On Memorial Day, 1932, in Yankee Stadium's center field, the Yankees placed the first of their famous Stadium monuments – in honor of Miller Huggins.

Huggins' final pennant in 1928 was his sixth. The Philadelphia A's owned first place when they visited Yankee Stadium September 9 for a doubleheader. They were swept, then beaten again the next day with the unheralded Hank Johnson besting the great Lefty Grove for the fifth time in five 1928 match-ups.

These Yankees led the league in batting, home runs, RBIs, hits, walks and slugging. They had four strong starting pitchers in Pipgras (24-13), Hoyt (23-7), Pennock (17-6) and Johnson (14-9). Ruth won the league home run title with 54, and he and Gehrig

Right: *Some of the reported 85,000 fans who saw the Yankees under Miller Huggins (in uniform, with A's manager Connie Mack) take a doubleheader from Philadelphia on September 9, 1928, to regain first place in the American League race. The right-field grandstands at Yankee Stadium had yet to be extended, leaving a huge bleacher area. Today Yankee Stadium, with its tidy bleachers, seats 57,545.*

(.374) shared the RBI title (142). Combs, the key table-setter, hit .310, scored 118 runs and led the league in triples with 21.

Earle Combs hit .325 lifetime, and scored over 100 runs every year from 1925 to 1932. He was known back home in Kentucky, where he had taught school before entering professional baseball, as "the fastest foot in the mountain country." He was a gentleman, and his achievements got a little lost sometimes, but with Combs began the Yankees' tradition of excellence in center field.

Once again the Yankees swept in the World Series. Yankee pitchers did what they had done a year earlier; they held the Nationals, this time St. Louis, to an average of two earned runs per game. But in the 1928 Series the feat was achieved by only three pitchers: Hoyt, with complete-game victories in games one and four, and Pipgras and Tom Zachary, who had complete-game wins in games two and three. Even such sterling mound performances as these were eclipsed by Ruth and Gehrig. Ruth hit .625, the highest average in Series history, and blasted three home runs in the final game; Gehrig had a .545 average, with four homers and nine RBIs.

The Yankees partied all the way from St. Louis. People flocked to their cars at each train stop to get a glimpse of the wonders of baseball.

The next year, 1929, the Yankees put numbers on their uniforms – Ruth's "3" and Gehrig's "4" became famous overnight – but the big number was 18, the 18 games Philadelphia won the pennant by. Connie Mack's A's were spectacular, with hitters like Al Simmons, Jimmie Foxx and Mickey Cochrane, and, on the mound, the incomparable Lefty Grove. And New York had problems. Joe Dugan was gone and the left side of the infield was weakened. The pitching was off, too. Johnson's season was ruined by a back injury, and Hoyt faltered and was traded the next season.

One bright spot was a 22-year-old rookie who hit .324 and had all the tools to become a great defensive catcher. Bill Dickey would catch at least 100 games for 13 consecutive seasons, setting a league record, and he "made catching look easy," in the words of Detroit's Charlie Gehringer, who made playing second base look easy. Dickey, who hit .313 lifetime with 202 homers, may have been the greatest all-round catcher ever.

New York in 1930 finished third under rookie manager Bob Shawkey, but Gehrig and Ruth were devastating. Gehrig, in his prime now (41 homers, .379 batting average), led the league in RBIs with 174, and Ruth (153 RBIs, .359 batting average) led in

Left: *They called the quiet and religious Earle Combs "The Kentucky Colonel" not because he came from the landed gentry, but because he was a gentleman. The handsome and fleet-footed man from the hill country was the tablesetter for Ruth and Gehrig. He hit a smart .325 over a dozen campaigns.*

homers with 49. Shawkey was harshly dumped following the season, Ruppert and Barrow leaping at the chance to hire the just-fired Cubs manager, Joe McCarthy.

So 1931 opened the era of Marse Joe McCarthy, 44, who had never played in the majors but who had won a pennant for the Chicago Cubs in 1929. The authoritarian McCarthy found himself ringed by a bunch of tough, rollicking ballplayers. Ruth set the tone, but with exceptions like Combs and Pennock aside, the entire team was capable of breaking training rules. Now here was McCarthy, having the clubhouse card table smashed to kindling.

Lazzeri wasn't amused when he happened to witness McCarthy's tongue-lashing of a teammate. But McCarthy won Lazzeri over by insisting that the player was cheating both his team and himself by not giving his best. Other veterans followed Lazzeri's lead, and the younger players followed the veterans. But Ruth could never accept McCarthy; he wanted McCarthy's job.

Well aware of Ruth's feelings, McCarthy

Above: *Lefty Gomez warming up. Gomez won 189 games for the New Yorkers between 1930 and 1942, and another half-dozen in World Series competition.*

danced around them. He accommodated to the two sets of rules he inherited – a loose-tether set for Ruth and another for everybody else. McCarthy's approach was to let well enough alone as long as Ruth's big bat produced. And it did. Marse Joe's job was certainly not threatened by the Babe – Ruppert and Barrow weren't convinced Ruth could manage *himself.*

Marse Joe finished second in 1931, 13 and a half games behind Philadelphia. His big hitter was Gehrig, who set the standing league record with 184 RBIs and tied Ruth for the league home run title with 46. And his two biggest winners on the mound were Lefty Gomez (21-9) and Red Ruffing (16-14). Funny, fun-loving Lefty Gomez, "The Gay Castillian" from sunny California, and Red Ruffing, a down-to-business athlete who had given four toes to an Illinois coal mine, formed a lefty-righty odd couple.

Gomez was skinny, a little goofy and a

terrible hitter. After Dickey talked with him on the mound about how to pitch to the great Foxx, Lefty confided, "I'd rather not throw the ball at all." Ruffing was solid and stolid and so good with the bat that he was used as a pinch hitter. A regular guy off the field, he was a cold fish when working. Together Gomez and Ruffing were the pitching core of the great New York teams of the 1930s: Gomez having 20 or more wins in 1931, 1932, 1934 and 1937, and Ruffing in 1936, 1937, 1938 and 1939.

The Yankees turned the tables on Philly in 1932, winning 107 games and running away from the A's. They would sweep the Cubs and extend their World Series winning streak to 12 games in an emotional Series. McCarthy wanted to sting his former employer, and his players were offended when former teammate Mark Koenig, now a Cub, was voted only a partial Series share. Ruth taunted the Cubs and the Cubs shot back. By the time the Series moved to Chicago for game three it was dripping with hostility. Ruth loved it.

It was after Chicago tied the score, 4-4, in game three that Ruth hit his "called shot" home run. The story goes that he pointed toward the bleachers after a called strike one. Strike two. Abuse streamed from the Cub dugout. Again he pointed. Then a long home run took flight along the route Ruth had indicated. Earle Combs was watching the Cubs in their dugout. "There they were – all out on the top step and yelling their brains out," Combs said, and when Ruth cracked the ball they "fell back as if they were being machine-gunned."

Eight members of this Yankee team – Ruth, Gehrig, Combs, Dickey, Gomez, Ruffing, Pennock and a former Indian, third baseman Joe Sewell – would enter the Hall of Fame. And Lazzeri, speedy outfielder Ben Chapman, pitcher Johnny Allen (17-4), Pipgras and shortstop Frank Crosetti, the lynchpin of the infield, were all top-drawer players.

The Yankees finished second in 1933, second in 1934, and second in 1935. Some of the writers began calling Marse Joe "Second-Place Joe." Pennock, at 39, pitched his last game in 1933, and Ruth, with Combs and Sewell just a few years his junior, was beginning to feel his 38 years. He was declining rapidly.

But the Babe did have a memorable October 1, 1933, when he took the mound and beat his old club, the Red Sox, helping his cause with his thirty-fourth homer. A year later, however, on September 30, 1934, Babe Ruth played his last game as a Yankee. The Yankees gave their franchise-maker an unconditional release to sign with the Boston Braves as a player-coach and club vice president. Ruth would find he didn't like the Boston arrangement, and he retired in June of 1935. Babe Ruth would never become a major-league manager.

The Yankees may have been stuck in second place but they had no second set of rules anymore. McCarthy preferred quiet, conservative players who followed the rules. Be champions and act like champions, he stressed, the latter exhortation requiring good conduct and dress decorum – a jacket and a tie.

Gehrig was the 1935 Yankees' superstar, having won the Triple Crown in the previous season for his three-way league leadership in homers (49), RBIs (165) and batting (.363). While his 1935 numbers, like the Yankee attendance figures, declined, he was the team's only legitimate power hitter. No matter what Gehrig did it never seemed enough. Someone, usually Ruth, and later, Joe DiMaggio, over-

shadowed his achievements. Did he receive the Most Valuable Player Award for his Triple-Crown 1934? No – the "someone else" this time was Mickey Cochrane of the pennant-winning Tigers.

George Selkirk, replacing Ruth in right field, had an excellent 1935 season (94 RBIs, .312 batting average), but a slugger was needed to help Gehrig and to fill the emotional void left by Ruth. The Yankees needed a Joe DiMaggio.

New York wasn't the only team interested in Joe, who in 1933 hit safely in 61 straight games for the San Francisco Seals. Much of the interest dampened when DiMaggio hurt a knee, but Yankee scouts fervently urged his acquisition, appealing over a balking Barrow directly to Ruppert. Persuaded, the owner made a deal with the Seals, a condition of which was that Joe would play one final year in San Francisco. Even so, Joe was only 21 when he arrived in New York in 1936 to help the Yankees win the pennant by a record 19 and a half games. He hit .323 with 29 homers, and set standing rookie records for the league in runs (132) and triples (15). He was one of five Yankees with more than 100 RBIs: Gehrig (152), DiMaggio (125), Lazzeri (109), Dickey (107), and Selkirk (107).

The Yankees in 1936 beat the New York Giants in the first Subway Series in 13 years. It took six games, a tough Series for the Yankees in those days. Over the next three seasons the Yankees were never challenged in the American League and in World Series competition defeated the Giants in five games in 1937, swept the Cubs in 1938 and swept the Reds in 1939. McCarthy's 1936-39 aggregation was truly awesome.

The Yankees put an exclamation point behind their fourth straight World Series

Below: *Two players who manager Joe McCarthy really leaned on – Joe DiMaggio, left, and Lou Gehrig. This photo was taken in 1939, the year Lou was forced to quit the game.*

Above: *The New York batboy greets Tony Lazzeri who has just homered in the 1937 World Series. Tony's .400 batting mark led his club to a World Championship – a great way to wrap up his final year with the Yankees. Frank Crosetti is on deck.*

Right: *Lazzeri in his sophomore year, 1927, showing his batting style.*

title when Charlie Keller flattened Reds catcher Ernie Lombardi on a play that netted three Yankee runs, as the dazed catcher "snoozed." Keller, a rookie, hit .438 in the Series. "Break up the Yankees, hell," complained a Reds fan with reference to a popular refrain. "I'll be satisfied if they just break up Keller." Keller was a product of the best farm system in baseball that was run in its smallest detail by George M. Weiss. New York's top farm club, the Newark Bears, in 1937 won the International League pennant by 25 games.

The heart and soul of the 1936-39 Yankees was DiMaggio, who in 1937 led the league in home runs (46) and in 1939 hit .381 to win the batting title. His RBIs over the four seasons ranged from 125 to 167.

One old hand to depart the Yankees following the 1937 season, making way for Joe Gordon, was Tony Lazzeri, the Yankees' first real Italian star. Lazzeri, who had seven 100-plus RBI seasons, was a tiger in the clutch.

Combined with Gomez and Ruffing were reliable starters Monte Pearson, Bump Hadley and Spud Chandler. Johnny

Murphy, a native New Yorker and a Fordham University star, was the game's premier reliever. Murphy accepted the role only after McCarthy promised to treat him at the pay window the same as the starters. Murphy was saving so many games for Gomez that the papers started referring to "Gomez-Murphy wins."

With his beloved Yankees riding high, Jake Ruppert should have been a contented man. But he seldom got to the Stadium in 1938 because of illness. Ruppert died on January 13, 1939, at the age of 71. The club passed to his estate and Barrow became club president.

While the Yankees as a team thundered, one Yankee fell off noticeably. Lou Gehrig was still powerful in 1938 (29 homers), but batted only .295. He got off slowly the next season and on May 2, 1939, asked to be taken out of the lineup. McCarthy hoped the warm weather of summer would bring him around. Lou was the kind of player McCarthy treasured. "He's always been a perfect gentleman, a credit to baseball," the manager said.

Gehrig was hitting only .143 and, as he related to his manager, he knew he was finished when Murphy complimented him for a routine play. For the first time since

June 1, 1925, the Iron Horse sat as the Yankees took the field, his then major-league record of 2,130 consecutive games brought to a close.

The entire nation was shocked weeks later when Gehrig handed Barrow a report from the Mayo Clinic saying that Lou was suffering from a form of infantile paralysis – amyotrophic lateral sclerosis – later to be known as Lou Gehrig Disease.

The Yankees held Lou Gehrig Appreciation Day on July 4, 1939, and among the old Yankees present was Babe Ruth. The Babe and Lou had had their differences, and he and Gehrig had not spoken in years, but on this occasion he impulsively threw his arms around Lou and hugged him. Gehrig told the Stadium crowd that although he was dealt a bad break he had much to live for. "Today I consider myself the luckiest man on the face of the earth," he said. Lou Gehrig died on June 2, 1941, two weeks before his thirty-eighth birthday.

Babe Dahlgren was Lou's competent 1939 replacement. He helped beat Detroit, 22-2, the day Lou benched himself. As the fact of the rout became obvious, he urged Lou to get in the game just to extend his streak. A smiling Gehrig told him: "No, you guys are doing OK without me."

Below: *July 4, 1939: Lou Gehrig listens to words of gratitude and praise during Lou Gehrig Appreciation Day ceremonies at Yankee Stadium. In a brief, moving speech Lou told the adoring crowd, "I may have been given a bad break, but I have an awful lot to live for. With all this, I consider myself the luckiest man on the face of this Earth."*

3. DiMag, the War, dem Bums

Below: *Marvelous rookie Phil Rizzuto, while mainly a glove man, batted .307 in 1941.*

Opposite: *Streaking around first base in Washington on June 29, 1941, is the focus of an entire nation, Joltin' Joe DiMaggio. On this twinbill day he tied and then broke George Sisler's consecutive-game hitting record of 41 games.*

In the 39 seasons between 1926 and 1964 the Yankees would finish as low as fourth only once, and that mediocre showing, in the war year of 1945, owed more to Adolph Hitler than to the rest of the American League.

They would finish as "low" as third only seven times, and one of those was in 1940 when they might have won it all had they been quicker to call pitcher Ernie "Tiny" Bonham up from their Kansas City farm team. Bonham arrived in August and won nine games with a 1.90 ERA. He was confined to nine wins the next year, but it didn't matter, the Yankees breezing to another pennant. These 1941 Yankees were blessed with fine performances turned in by Joe DiMaggio (30 homers, 125 RBIs, .357 batting average), Charlie Keller (33 homers, 122 RBIs), and Tommy Henrich (31 homers, 85 RBIs) – one of the all-time great outfields.

Henrich had joined the club in 1937, a year after DiMag. The Massillon, Ohio, native loved baseball and loved the

Yankees; the New York fans, in turn, loved "Old Reliable," a fine hitter, a great clutch hitter and an outstanding defensive outfielder. Left fielder Keller, on DiMaggio's other side, was also an accomplished outfielder, and so awesome was his power that when he had been with the Newark Bears he was compared with fellow Marylander Babe Ruth. Keller was intense and perfectionistic about his game.

Up the middle the Yankees had rookie Phil Rizzuto (.307) doing acrobatics at shortstop and the stylish Joe Gordon (24 homers, 87 RBIs) at second base, the two making many double plays which were welcomed by pitchers Ruffing, Gomez, Marius Russo, Spud Chandler and reliever Johnny Murphy.

Little Phil Rizzuto was spurned by both his hometown Brooklyn Dodgers and the New York Giants, then got his chance with the Yankees organization after impressing McCarthy and head scout Paul Krichell. He was the best bunter in the game, an excellent baserunner and the greatest Yankee shortstop ever, and, when his playing career ended in 1956, he continued his association with the club as a broadcaster. "Holy Cow!" – his exclamation for the unusual or spectacular – has long been the broadcast trademark of the personable Scooter.

The 1941 season had a start that was as bad as its ending was good. On May 15 the Yankees sustained their eighth defeat in 10 games. It was a day on which DiMaggio happened to get a hit. The next day he cracked a homer and a triple, and the day after that he singled, and the Yankee Clipper was off on a hitting streak. The streak grew and grew as a breathless nation watched Joe push toward the American League record of George Sisler, set with the Browns in 1922, of 41 straight games, and Willie Keeler's string of 44 games, set in 1897 when Keeler played for Baltimore of the National League. Almost forgotten, Keeler's streak was nevertheless the all-time record. DiMaggio smashed both records and kept on streaking. Finally, on July 17, before more than 67,000 in Cleve-

even in game four at Ebbets Field. The Dodgers were on track, leading 4-3 with two outs in the ninth and with two strikes on Henrich. Hugh Casey got strike three but the ball eluded catcher Mickey Owen, allowing Henrich to reach first. Then a single, double, walk and another double beat the Dodgers, 7-4. The next day the poor Bums could manage only five hits off Bonham. The final-game victory capped a remarkable string of 32 wins for the Yankees in 36 World Series games, dating back to 1927.

Things could not have been better for Joe McCarthy, who now had his sixth World Championship. Some saw McCarthy as lucky – successful only because he had the horses – but one man regarded him as the greatest manager in history. And Ed Barrow wasn't alone. "Never a day went by when you didn't learn something from McCarthy," Joe DiMaggio once said.

McCarthy, however, *was* blessed. In 1942 his power-hitting second baseman, Joe Gordon – as flashy a second sacker as there ever was – knocked in 103 runs, hit .322 and won the league's MVP Award. Gordon, who was signed out of the University of Oregon,

Right: *Joe Gordon had a fine first year in 1938 as Tony Lazzeri's replacement, hitting 25 homers and rapping home 97 runs. After serving seven seasons at second base for New York, Gordon went to Cleveland in the Allie Reynolds trade.*

Above: *The Dodgers' Mickey Owen chases a ball that was strike three with two outs in the ninth inning of game four of the 1941 World Series. Tommy Henrich reached and the Yanks, down 4-3, rallied to win and dent the Dodgers' hopes by going up 3-1 in the Series.*

land's Municipal Stadium, and with third baseman Ken Keltner making two great plays on balls off DiMaggio's bat, the streak that captivated a nation, and revived the Yankees, ended at 56 games!

The Yankees finished 17 games in front of the closest competition. Now they would face Dem Bums, the Dodgers, in the first of seven World Series parings with Brooklyn extending through 1956. The Yankees went up two games to one in that 1941 Series and the Dodgers wanted desperately to pull

would play in 1000 Yankee games and have exactly 1000 hits, 153 of them homers. He was the premier second baseman in the American League for a decade. In 1942 McCarthy also had the league's best pitching staff, led by Bonham (21-5). The Yanks also had the best fielding team, the key to which was the up-the-middle defense of catcher Bill Dickey, second baseman Gordon, shortstop Rizzuto and center fielder DiMaggio.

Having run away with the American

Left: *Safe at first is Snuffy Stirnweiss. He had tapped a slow roller and elected to slide in this 1944 game with the A's in Philadelphia's Shibe Park. Irv Hall, number 6, was there but first baseman Dick Siebert tried to beat the Yankees' 1944 star to the bag. Pitcher Bo Bo Newsom watches in the background.*

League flag and with a history of spectacular World Series successes, the Yankees were not exactly quivering as they faced the young St. Louis Cardinals in the 1942 World Series. The teams split the first two games, but game three was to prove a backbreaker. The Cardinals won behind inspired play in the outfield, Terry Moore robbing DiMaggio of a triple, Stan Musial stealing a home run from Gordon, and Enos Slaughter leaping to snatch another potential homer off Keller's bat. The Cardinals went on to win the World Championship.

Meanwhile, the nation was at war after the December 7, 1941 attack on Pearl Harbor. Baseball, however, would be played not only in 1942 but throughout World War II. The Yankees, even with DiMaggio, Rizzuto, Henrich and Ruffing in the military, again won the pennant in 1943. They *did* have Spud Chandler (20-4), winner of the 1943 MVP Award. Chandler, who had been a three-sport star at the University of Georgia, led the league in wins (20), winning percentage (.833), complete games (20), shutouts (5) and ERA (1.64). Chandler's .717 lifetime winning percentage is still the highest in major-league history for pitchers with at least 100 lifetime decisions; Spud was 109-43 lifetime.

Again in the 1943 World Series the Yankees were pitted against the Cardinals,

but this time it was New York that came out on top. Fittingly, Chandler won the fifth and final game with a shutout, winning 2-0 on Dickey's two-run homer.

However, the "wartime Yankees" fell off markedly, the club finishing third in 1944 and fourth in 1945. The team's number one star was Snuffy Stirnweiss. The son of a New York City policeman, Stirnweiss learned baseball on the sandlots of the Bronx and refined his skills at the University of North Carolina. He was fast, and as a Yankee he was an exciting and popular infielder who played mostly at second base. He had a spectacular 1945, leading the league in batting (.309), slugging (.476), runs (107), hits (195), triples (22), and stolen bases (33).

The war was still raging on January 25, 1945, when the Ruppert heirs sold the team to Larry MacPhail, Dan Topping and Del Webb. The incoming threesome were modern businessmen; two-fisted "Cousin Ed" Barrow was not. Admittedly old-fashioned, Barrow was as conservative as he was tough. He disdained night baseball and promotions. The only show that mattered to him was baseball. MacPhail, who became the Yankees' president and general manager, with Barrow going upstairs as board chairman, saw things far differently. He was as pro-night ball as Barrow was pro-

Right: *In 1943 the American League's MVP was Spud Chandler. After serving in World War II, Chandler returned and at the age of 39 won 20 games for New York in 1946. He had an incredible .717 lifetime winning percentage.*

sunshine, having pioneered the night game with Cincinnati in 1935. He was a promoter and he promoted. When Barrow, at 79, got his fill of the models in jeeps and the barbershop quartets, he "quit and went home," as he put it in his autobiography.

MacPhail was daring and individualistic. As a World War I captain, he had been part of a failed enterprise to capture Kaiser Wilhelm of Germany. In his brief three years with the Yankees he revitalized the franchise and brought excitement to New York. He was innovative and bright, but he was bombastic and pugnacious and had disagreements with many.

McCarthy didn't feel comfortable working for MacPhail, and his health began to suffer. On May 24, 1946, Joe McCarthy resigned. It would be a three-manager season: McCarthy, Dickey and Johnny Neun. The team finished third, even with the regulars back from the military.

But in 1947, under Manager Bucky Harris, New York moved into first place on June 19 and stayed there. DiMaggio, now 32 but back in form, won his third MVP Award, an honor based more on what Joe meant to the Yankees than on his personal statistics, which were good but not great. DiMaggio, who hit .315 with 20 homers, was a lot more than a hitter and, in fact, led

all league outfielders with a .997 fielding percentage. He was an excellent baserunner, a heads-up player who never missed a sign, a leader and a ballhawking center fielder with a great arm. Even in a year when he didn't post his best offensive numbers, he was still deemed to be the "most valuable," and many still consider him to have been baseball's all-time most complete player.

The 1947 Yankees had another star in pitcher Allie Reynolds (19-8), acquired in a trade that sent Joe Gordon to Cleveland. They also had reliever Joe Page, Murphy's successor, who collected 17 saves to lead the league. The infield included 38-year-old first baseman George McQuinn, who was picked up as a free agent and hit .304, Stirnweiss at second, Rizzuto at shortstop and Billy Johnson (95 RBIs) at third. The outfield was a little unsettled, what with Keller out most of the season with a back injury, but Henrich drove in 98 runs and DiMaggio 97. And catcher Yogi Berra was starting to hit pretty well in this, his second, year. The seven-game engagement with Brooklyn was one of the most exciting World Series ever, and Dodgers fans had plenty to cheer about, especially in game four. The Yankees' Bill Bevens had a no-hitter for eight and two-thirds innings.

Then Bevens walked Carl Furillo, and Furillo's pinch runner, Al Gionfriddo, stole second base. Harris ordered an intentional pass to Pete Reiser, and pinch hitter Cookie Lavagetto belted a double, winning it for the Bums, 3-2, and breaking up Bevens' no-hit bid. The unheralded Gionfriddo also made a great catch of a screaming drive off DiMaggio's bat to save game six for Brooklyn. However, the Yankees won game seven behind Page, who allowed only one hit over the final five innings.

It was a great team effort and everyone was ecstatic, everyone, that is, except Larry MacPhail. It had been a rough year for MacPhail, who became involved in disputes with the Dodgers in spring training, leading to a year's suspension for Dodgers manager Leo Durocher (which hadn't been Larry's intention), and an irreparable falling-out with Dodgers boss Branch Rickey, which he tried unsuccessfully to patch up during the Series.

MacPhail, who was temperamental all season and not a popular man around the Yankees, was simply wild at the Series victory party. He insulted several people (including at least one Yankee player), punched a former employee, angrily fired farm director George Weiss and argued with his partners, Topping and Webb. The next day Webb and Topping bought out MacPhail for $2 million and named Weiss general manager. Everyone was happy to see MacPhail go, perhaps forgetting that the Yankees had made more money in MacPhail's three years than any other team had made in 10 years.

Although a new era dawned for the Yankees in 1948, the overriding event was the passing of the franchise-maker. Babe

Ruth died of throat cancer at 53 on August 16, not long after his final Stadium appearance. The weather on the day Babe was buried was brutally hot, nudging Joe Dugan, the old third baseman, to confess to fellow pallbearer Waite Hoyt that he'd give his "right arm for a beer." To which Hoyt answered, "So would the Babe."

The Yankees in 1948 finished third but were not eliminated from the race until the next-to-last day of the season. However, Harris was having problems with general manager George Weiss. Weiss felt the team lacked discipline and that this defect could be attributed to Harris, whom Weiss often couldn't reach. Bucky, known as "the four-hour manager," was always "out" when Weiss called. On October 6, 1948, Harris was fired. Harris was shocked. On October 12, 1948, Casey Stengel was announced as the new manager. The baseball world was shocked. Daffy Casey Stengel?

Above: *The Ruppert era ends. In 1945 the Ruppert heirs sold the Yankees to three partners, Del Webb, Dan Topping and Col. Larry MacPhail. Here Webb (left) and MacPhail (right) huddle with club president Ed Barrow in a New York eatery.*

Below left: *Thousands of people waited on long lines outside Yankee Stadium to pass before the bier of Babe Ruth, whose body lay in state about 200 feet from the home plate where the Babe made baseball history. His death on August 16, 1948 marked the end of an era.*

4. You Think I was Born Old?

Daffy Casey Stengel would reel off five World Championships in a row, out-doing even Joe McCarthy's great string of four.

When Stengel joined the Yankees, he was well-known in baseball, having been in the game professionally since 1910 and having served as a solid .284 hitter with five National League teams, among them Brooklyn and the Giants of John McGraw. He was well-liked, but after joining the managerial ranks, he was not necessarily well-respected. The Brooklyn and Boston Braves teams he managed in the 1930s and early 1940s were terrible. He was known for his clownishness. Babe Ruth called him "one of the daffiest guys I ever met." He enjoyed entertaining people, like the time when he came to the plate, tipped his cap – and out flew a bird.

But general manager George Weiss wanted Casey. Weiss felt he could work with Stengel, and the two indeed were to make a powerful team. But they were dissimilar types. Casey was outgoing and colorful, Weiss drab and humorless. Weiss was a suspicious sort who used Stengel as a buffer, particularly with the press, but he was brilliant as Yankees farm director (1932-47). "Lonesome George," who pinched pennies so hard Lincoln looked like Churchill, would do just as well as general manager (1948-60). Owner Del Webb, a construction tycoon, was a great fan with good baseball instincts, but basically, he and co-owner Dan Topping allowed Weiss and Stengel to run the show.

Stengel, ushered into the Hall of Fame in 1966, was the single most visible Yankee in the 1949-60 era, but not all sides of this complex man were readable. Those the public saw were conveyed by reporters who thought the world of him. He came across as a kindly, humorous man – and he was – but he also had a sharpness to him that only his players saw.

Casey's language was something called Stengelese. In 1958 a U.S. Senate subcommittee considering the exemption of professional sports from anti-trust laws held hearings and invited Stengel to testify. He was asked: "How many minor leagues were there when you broke into baseball?" His reply:

Well, there were not so many at that time because of this fact: Anybody to go into baseball at that time with the educational schools that we had were small, while you were probably thoroughly educated at school, you had to be – we had only small cities that you could put a team in and they would go defunct.

Why, I remember the first year I was at Kankakee, Illinois, and a bank offered me $500 if I would let them have a little notice. I left there and took a uniform because they owed me two weeks' pay. But I either had to quit – but I did not have enough money to go to dental college – so I had to go with the manager down to Kentucky.

What happened there was if you got by

Below: *The Yankees' hard-throwing relief pitcher, Joe Page, in 1949 – the year he had 27 saves and was a key factor in the New York Yankees' World Championship season.*

Left: *What's in store? That question might well have been on the mind of the Yankees' new manager, Casey Stengel, as he surveyed Yankee Stadium in this 1948 photo. He would prove to be a great, albeit improbable, choice as manager.*

July, that was the big date. You did not play night ball and you did not play Sundays in half of the cities on account of a Sunday observance, so in those days when things were tough, and all of it was, I mean to say, why they just closed up July 4 and there you were sitting there in the depot. You could go to work some place else, but that was it. So I got out of Kankakee and I just go there for the visit now.

In 1949, his first year as Yankee manager, Stengel took an injury-plagued team – DiMaggio, for one, was sidelined half the season – to the pinnacle of baseball. The Yankees were trailing front-running Boston by one game when the Red Sox came to the Bronx for the season's final two games. The Yanks, with key hits by Johnny Lindell and Jerry Coleman, won both. New York then prevailed in a five-game World Series against Brooklyn. The World Series

MVP, pitcher Joe Page, closed the Series by striking out Duke Snider, Jackie Robinson and Gil Hodges.

Page, signed off the sandlots of western Pennsylvania, was up and down with the Yankees, but for two seasons, 1947 and 1949, he was awesome. Yankees fans loved to see Page, the first reliever to use the strikeout as a trump card, blow fastballs by the hitters. He saved so many games for Reynolds that the press, as it had referred to Gomez-Murphy wins in an earlier era, wrote of Reynolds-Page victories.

Most of the writers and experts picked Boston to win the 1950 pennant, but the Yankees again claimed the flag. Joe DiMaggio enjoyed his final great year (32 homers, 122 RBIs, .301 batting average), but the Yankees were led offensively by Phil Rizzuto, known more for his great defensive play at shortstop. This was little

Great Yankees pitching included Vic Raschi's two-hitter in the opener and rookie Whitey Ford's final-game effort. Ford had a shutout going with two outs in the ninth when a fly ball hid in the autumn haze from left fielder Gene Woodling, opening the door for a couple of Philly runs before Reynolds closed it.

Brought up in mid-season, Ford was an important factor in the Yankees' 1950 success, winning all but one of his 10 decisions. He was destined to be the biggest winner in Yankees history, with a club-record 236 victories. If he hadn't made it in baseball, the Queens native might have been a nice, accommodating New York cop. He was good-natured, and he was funny. When teammate Hank Bauer introduced the future Hall of Famer to a fellow Marine, who like Bauer wore a face with the topographical interest of the Great Plains, Whitey wondered, "What'd you guys fight the war with anyway? Shovels?"

The pitching continued to lead the way in the regular season of 1951. Vic Raschi and Eddie Lopat each won 21 games, Raschi for the third straight season. Remarkably, Allie Reynolds (17-8) pitched no-hitters against Cleveland on July 12 and against Boston on September 28. In the second no-hitter, catcher Yogi Berra dropped the final out on a foul pop, but held on when Ted Williams popped up to him a second time.

Above: *The beginning of the end – the first pitch by Whitey Ford in game four of the 1950 World Series against the Phillies. The Yankees won, 5-2, to sweep the Series. Eddie Waitkus is at bat and Yogi Berra is catching.*

Right: *Another great Yankee pitcher, Allie Reynolds, is mobbed by happy teammates on July 12, 1951, after his no-hitter against Cleveland. The Yanks won, 1-0.*

Phil's big year at the plate (.324 batting average with 200 hits – 36 of them doubles – and 125 runs scored) for which he won the league MVP Award.

It was the Whiz Kids, the Philadelphia Phillies, in the 1950 Fall Classic, and the Kids were swept – 1-0, 2-1, 3-2 and 5-2.

Reynolds, Raschi and Lopat were the Big Three of New York moundsmen for the

1949-53 period. Lopat, a lefty and a native New Yorker, used a variety of off-speed offerings. Raschi was a thrower; he threw hard, and he threw himself into every game he pitched. Reynolds was a right-handed power pitcher who worked as a reliever as well as a starter. Stengel liked to serve power-finesse-power sandwiches: Raschi-Lopat-Reynolds.

The year 1951 was a transitional year for the Yankees. Joe DiMaggio (12 homers, 71 RBIs) played his final season, and Mickey Mantle (13 homers, 65 RBIs), a promising, rookie switch hitter, played in 96 games.

Mantle was not the only good-looking rookie. It was Gil McDougald who won the Rookie of the Year Award. McDougald was a remarkably versatile infielder; he remains the only player in Yankees history to be a regular at second base (three years), shortstop (two years) and third base (three years). The San Franciscan agreed to play at third when first asked, quipping that the hitters couldn't do any more than "knock my teeth out."

The 1951 World Series pitting the Yankees against the New York Giants started well for the Giants, who had made a miracle comeback to nose out Brooklyn for the National League pennant. They had the Yankees down two games to one when a day of rain intervened, allowing Stengel to bring back Reynolds for game four. With the help of a two-run DiMaggio homer, Reynolds won, 6-2. Lopat won game five, his second victory of the Series, and the Yankees led in game six, 4-1, as the Giants came to bat in the top of the ninth. The Giants knocked the ball all over the big ball field, and had two more runs rung up when right fielder Hank Bauer recorded the final out, diving for a slicing liner and grabbing the ball inches from the Stadium turf.

DiMaggio had doubled in the eighth inning of this deciding game. It was his last at-bat in baseball, and when he was thrown out at third in a bunt attempt to move him over, the crowd rose to cheer Joe. On December 11, 1951, Joltin' Joe DiMaggio retired from baseball, at the age of 37.

And now there was another Yankee showing signs of becoming a storied star. When scout Tom Greenwade first saw Mickey Mantle playing ball in Oklahoma, he knew how Yankees scout Paul Krichell "must have felt the first time he saw Lou Gehrig." Mickey possessed tremendous power from both sides of the plate, blinding speed and a great arm. However, the kid wasn't the shortstop he set out to be and Casey converted him to an outfielder. A former outfielder himself, Stengel helped teach him the position, once taking him to the Ebbets Field outfield before an exhibition game to show him how to play the tricky right-field wall. "Gee, Casey, I didn't know you played here," a surprised Mantle blurted. "For crissakes," the manager complained, "you think I was born old?"

Mickey's 1951 season had its rocky moments. He was only 19 and had been heavily reported in a spring training in which he blasted some majestic home runs. The fans were led to believe he was Babe Ruth and Ty Cobb rolled into one.

Below: *Mickey Mantle in his first game as a Yankee, April 17, 1951. Mickey had 13 homers in his first year, well below the expectations of many. He is wearing the number 6 here; later he would take the number 7.*

football. So Mickey had to deal with unbridled expectations on the one hand and unreasonable resentment on the other.

With DiMaggio gone, Mickey in 1952 moved from right field to center and came into his own, hitting .311 with 23 homers. Between 1952 and 1955, Mantle averaged 27 homers and 95 RBIs a season, and Yogi Berra averaged 26.5 homers and 101 RBIs. They were the twin guns, but it was Berra who won the MVP Award in 1951, 1954 and 1955.

Berra, a squat 5'8", didn't look like an athlete, yet was a standout. The future Hall of Famer was, to Stengel, "a great man." He was not only an exceptional catcher and hitter, but he had a way about him – and a way with words – that made him known to millions who didn't know the difference between home plate and the water cooler. He would utter pearls, like, "You can see a lot by observing."

Yogi went almost two seasons, from mid-1957 to early 1959, without an error behind the plate, and he was a masterful handler of pitchers. As one of the game's most feared hitters, especially in the late innings, he would surprise pitchers by chasing bad pitches, but his ability to connect was no surprise. He struck out only 12 times in 1950, one of his five 100-plus RBI seasons.

The Yankees defeated Brooklyn in both the 1952 and 1953 World Series. In game seven of the 1952 Series, Mantle homered to break a 2-2 tie, and then singled in a run to give the Yankees a 4-2 lead. The Dodgers loaded the bases with two outs in the bottom of the seventh, and Stengel allowed the left-handed Bob Kuzava to pitch to the right-handed Jackie Robinson. Robinson hit a high infield pop-up. A wind played with the ball as the Dodgers streaked around the bases, and, just when it seemed the ball would drop safely in the seemingly frozen infield, second baseman Billy Martin raced in to make a lunging catch. Kuzava pitched hitless ball the rest of the way and the Yankees again were the World Champs.

Martin led the Yankees in the six-game 1953 Series, banging 12 hits for a .500 average, driving in eight runs, and giving Stengel, with whom he felt a special bond, the record fifth straight World Championship. Billy capped his great overall performance by singling home the winning run in the bottom of the ninth of the final game. "Billy was wonderful," Casey beamed, "really magnificent." Stengel loved the aggressive, scrappy Billy. He encouraged him to be even more aggressive. There was to be a day when DiMaggio would be named to manage the Yankees and a gravely ill Casey would weep with joy.

Right: *Whew! No one was going after Jackie Robinson's pop fly in the deciding game of the 1952 World Series until Billy Martin raced in to make the grab. The catch ended a late-inning Dodgers rally and the Yanks went on to win, 4-2. Wishing the charging second baseman the best is the Yanks' shortstop, Phil Rizzuto.*

Naturally, the impossible was expected of him. He was no DiMaggio, New Yorkers soon decided. And why wasn't this strongman in the Army? The answer was that the Army didn't want him. He had osteomyelitis, a bone disease contracted after being kicked in the leg while playing high school

Left: *Yogi Berra was a great hitter, a great catcher and a great athlete who, as a Yankee from 1946 through 1963, was good most seasons for 20 to 30 home runs.*

Stengel and Weiss were able to keep together a solid nucleus on all five World Championship teams that included Berra, Rizzuto, Bauer, Woodling, Reynolds, Lopat, Raschi, Coleman, Johnny Mize and first baseman Joe Collins. And they filled holes effectively. When a good defensive outfielder was needed, a trade was swung with Washington for Irv Noren. When Bobby Brown retired to turn to medicine, Andy Carey took over at third base and did the job. To plug a hole in the bullpen, Johnny Sain, the Boston Braves' star, was obtained for Lew Burdette and cash.

The pennant string was broken in 1954 even though the Yankees won 103 games (Cleveland won 111), but in 1955 the Yankees climbed back to the top. They had a balanced pitching staff, an infield of Bill "Moose" Skowron at first, McDougald at second, and Carey at third, with Billy Hunter and an aging Rizzuto sharing shortstop. Berra was behind the plate. Center fielder Mantle was flanked by Bauer and Noren, and a key reserve was rookie Elston Howard.

Howard was the Yankees' first black player, arriving eight years after Jackie Robinson broke in with Brooklyn. Larry MacPhail had instituted a system for scouting black baseball but his efforts were blunted by a George Weiss who wanted black and white on his uniforms but not in them. Stengel, though occasionally guilty of insensitive remarks on the matter of race, made Howard feel at home all the same. And so did the Yankees players, Rizzuto in particular. Howard in time would be more than accepted; he would be respected both as a man and player.

The 1955 World Series was the one that Brooklyn at long last was able to win. The Yankees had two on in the sixth inning of game seven when Berra hit a long, slicing drive that Sandy Amoros speared in the left-field corner. Then Amoros doubled up a baserunner in a saving play for Brooklyn, who went on to win the game, 2-0, and the Series.

New York and Brooklyn faced each other again in the 1956 World Series. Powered by two homers from Berra and one each from Howard and Skowron, the Yankees won the seventh and deciding game, 9-0, behind Johnny Kucks' three-hitter. But this was not the pitching masterpiece of the 1956 Series.

Don Larsen made baseball history in

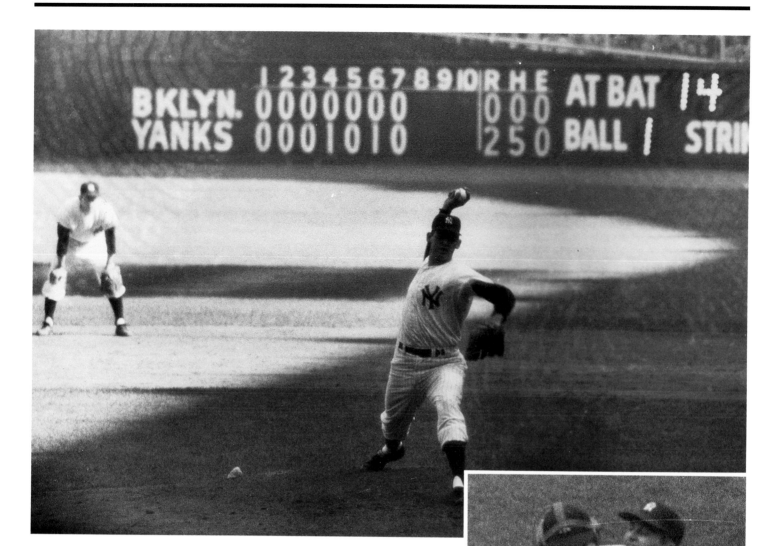

	1 2 3 4 5 6 7 8 9 10	R H E	AT BAT	14
BKLYN.	0 0 0 0 0 0 0	0 0 0	BALL 1	STRI
YANKS	0 0 0 1 0 1 0	2 5 0		

Above: *On the way to a perfect game – the first ever in World Series competition – is Don Larsen of the New York Yankees. The date is October 8, 1956.*

Right: *Larsen does it! Catcher Yogi Berra shows his appreciation for the historic achievement. The Yankees beat the Dodgers, 2-0.*

game five at Yankee Stadium by pitching a perfect game. It was three up and three down for nine innings, the only no-hitter in World Series history, and major-league baseball's first perfect game in three and a half decades. The biggest defensive play in Larsen's behalf came when Mantle raced into deep left center to make a back-handed grab of Gil Hodges' smoking liner. The year 1956 not only produced Larsen's remarkable achievement but marked the emergence of Mickey Mantle as the best player in the game. Leading the league in batting (.353), homers (52) and RBIs (130), Mantle became only the second Yankee ever, after Gehrig, to win the Triple Crown. The league MVP for the year also led the league in slugging (.705) and runs (132).

The Yankees in 1957 would again win the pennant. They were winning pennants with annoying regularity, swelling the Legion of Yankee Haters' ranks. This year the Milwaukee Braves, and not Brooklyn, would be their World Series foe. The Yankees would never again face the Brooklyn Dodgers, or, for that matter, the New York Giants. Both teams vacated the City of New York for California with the close of the 1957 season. Would the Yankees, with the huge New York market all to themselves, enjoy unprecedented prosperity?

No. Not in the short haul, at least. The market was so poisoned by the two clubs' pull-out that the Yankees' home attendance actually dipped in 1958 to 1,428,428, down by about 70,000 from the previous year.

The Braves in the 1957 World Series had Lew Burdette, the pitcher acquired in the Sain deal who happened to have been developed in the Yankees' farm system, and Burdette was enough. He creamed his old organization, winning games two, five and seven. The Braves were the new World Champions.

The Yankees in 1958 recorded a modest 92 wins – 21 of them posted by Cy Young Award winner Bob Turley – but finished first comfortably. Milwaukee again won the Nationals' flag, and in the World Series rematch had the Yankees on the ropes, three games to one, and with Burdette ready to start game five. But Turley five-hit the Braves to snap Burdette's Series winning streak at four games. Then New York emerged a 4-3 victor from a 10-inning struggle and the stage was set for the deciding game.

A four-run rally in the eighth, featuring a three-run homer by Skowron, put game seven into the Yankees' column, 6-2. The losing pitcher was Burdette, and the winning pitcher was Turley. After being driven from the mound in a humiliating 13-5 defeat in game two, "Bullet Bob" Turley, of Troy, Illinois, proved to be the comeback hero, winning twice and saving another game in this great comeback Series for the Yankees. Turley, Larsen and Ryne Duren, New York's winning hurlers, got help from Bauer (four homers, eight RBIs), Skowron (two homers, seven RBIs) and McDougald (two homers, four RBIs). What made the victory all the more satisfying – beyond the avenging of 1957's defeat – was its payback for uncomplimentary remarks by a few of the Braves when it looked like New York was all but beaten for the second year in a row. Reflected Milwaukee shortstop Johnny Logan: "Their determination beat us. Determination and Yankee Pride."

One familiar Yankee did not share in the joy of the 1958 comeback. Billy Martin, after figuring in a much-publicized altercation in Manhattan's Copacabana Club in 1957, was traded to Kansas City. Weiss disliked Martin and felt he was a bad influence on Yankee stars. It wouldn't be the last time Billy would get the heave-ho from Yankee management. He would be okay with Yankee fans, however – and for a long time to come.

Left: *Catcher Elston Howard (left) with the 1958 Babe Ruth Award and pitcher Bob Turley with the 1958 Cy Young Award. They led the Yanks to the great comeback victory over the Braves in the 1958 World Series.*

5. The Rich Get Richer – to a Point

The heroes of the thrilling and satisfying comeback victory over the Milwaukee Braves in the 1958 World Series got off to a poor start in 1959, then, on May 20, actually sank to the cellar. The Yankees would recover, but not enough to seriously challenge the pennant-winning White Sox. New York actually won only four games more than they lost (79-75), finishing 15 games behind Chicago. The numbers for all the Yankees power hitters were down, and the pitchers had off-years, too. The final straw was the July 25 injury to first baseman Bill Skowron. Reaching for a bad throw, Skowron suffered a broken arm in two places when a baserunner cracked into him. It was one of those the-year-the-Yankees-didn't-win-the-pennant years.

But that wouldn't be the case the next year, 1960, when the Yankees won their tenth pennant in Casey Stengel's 12 seasons as manager. After a summer-long battle with Chicago and Baltimore, the Yankees finished strong and were eight games in front at the season's close. They wrapped it up with a 15-game winning streak that brought their record to 97-57.

It was the first Yankees season of Roger Maris, obtained in an off-season trade with Kansas City, and the first full season of the superb infield of Skowron at first, Bobby Richardson at second, Tony Kubek at short and Clete Boyer at third.

Maris produced real power. The Gold Glove right fielder hit 39 homers and led the league in RBIs (112) and slugging (.581). He and Mickey Mantle formed the most productive power-hitting duo since Ruth and Gehrig. Mickey led the league in homers (40) and runs scored (119). Skowron also had a productive year (26 homers, 91 RBIs, .309 batting average). Yogi Berra was still contributing in a lesser role.

It was a solid offensive and defensive

Right: *Yogi Berra is congratulated by teammates after his sixth-inning home run put the Yankees up 5-4 in game seven of the 1960 World Series with the Pirates. Berra seems pensive, and maybe for good reason, for this was the game of the Mazeroski homer – the ninth-inning blast that won the World Championship for Pittsburgh.*

team with the league's best pitching staff, which was deep, though seemingly without an ace, and led by starters Art Ditmar (15-9), Jim Coates (13-3) and Whitey Ford (12-9), who had arm problems throughout the year. Awaiting the Yankees in the 1960 World Series, a Series that would prove to be one of the most memorable ever, was Pittsburgh.

The Yankees' wins in this Series were big wins, 16-3, 10-0 and 12-0. The Pirates' wins, going into the final, deciding game, were little wins, 6-4, 3-2 and 5-2. New York's two shutouts were pitched by Ford, and the Yankees might have had him on the mound for the finale had Stengel pitched Whitey in the opener. But Stengel in the first game had gone with his big winner on the year, Ditmar, who was shelled in the first inning and lost, 6-4. While pitching only one and two-thirds innings in the Series, Ditmar lost two games.

Game seven was played at Forbes Field. The Yankees were down by four runs when Skowron made it 4-1 with a homer in the fifth. In the sixth, a Berra homer led the Yankees in a four-run uprising that gave New York a 5-4 edge. The Yankees added two more in the eighth to form a 7-4 advantage. The Pirates made noises in the bottom of the eighth and then a potential double-play grounder took a wild hop off a rocky in-field and struck Kubek in the throat; all hands were safe and Kubek was removed from the field, requiring hospitalization. Dick Groat then singled in a run and Stengel removed left-handed Bobby Shantz, who had been pitching well since the third inning, and replaced him with the right-handed Coates even though the two Pirates due up were left-handed hitters. Coates retired both. But Roberto Clemente beat out a weak chopper that scored another run, and the score was 7-6. Hal Smith soon changed that, hitting a three-run homer to give the Pirates a 9-7 lead.

The Yankees fought back in the ninth, putting runners on first and third. Mantle then singled in a run, but when Berra bounced a one-out grounder to first baseman Rocky Nelson, the Pirates smelled a double play and victory. However, when Nelson touched the bag before going to second for the double play, Mantle, realizing that first base was now open, returned safely to the bag. The twin killing was thwarted and the tying run scored. It was 9-9.

However, Mantle's smart play was drowned out by the blast heard 'round the baseball world in the bottom of the ninth, the dramatic Bill Mazeroski home run off Ralph Terry that sent the people of Pittsburgh into the streets in joyous celebration.

Left: *The ace of the Yankees' pitching staff in 1960 with a record of 15-9, Art Ditmar had a tough time in the World Series that year. He not only lost two games to the Pirates, but he also only lasted a total of one and two-thirds innings.*

All left fielder Berra could do was helplessly watch the ball sail over the wall. Stengel took the loss badly but never blamed Terry, who was up in the bullpen at least four times and might have lost something by the time he got into the game.

A few days later Casey Stengel "retired" as Yankee manager, but not without wandering from the script co-owners Dan Topping and Del Webb had prepared. "I guess this means they fired me," said Casey. "I'll never make the mistake of being 70 again." But Weiss didn't make that mistake; he was only 66 and the Yankees let him go, too.

The Yankees had jettisoned a top-notch baseball manager. Casey Stengel, who had his origins in McGraw, was a great instiller of team confidence, a great deployer of base-ball ability and a great think-ahead manager in the dugout. And he was more. He was an engaging baseball personality, a marvelous ambassador for the game. He was the kind of warm-blooded, rough-featured old man that could give even the

Right: *The great Casey Stengel, who "retired" at the age of 70 after the 1960 season.*

Center: *Roger Maris, right, the American League's MVP in both 1960 and 1961, poses with the runner-up in both years, teammate Mickey Mantle.*

relentlessly ambitious and machine-like Yankees a touch of humanity. His retirement was not welcomed and the forced nature of it did not sit well with Yankees fans and the press.

The Yankees had someone waiting in the wings; the new man at the helm would be Ralph Houk. After catching a few games with the Yankees, Houk remained with the organization and became manager of the Denver farm club. At Denver, he won the Little World Series in 1957 and was credited with helping the development of Kubek, Richardson and others. He joined the Yankees in 1958 as a coach and, as Topping's man, heir apparent to Stengel. Houk, eternally optimistic, praise-generous and tough, had risen to the rank of major in World War II and earned a Silver Star. Houk's philosophy in deploying his players was different from Stengel's. Houk believed in a set team and a regular rotation for his pitchers, and for this, won instant rapport with his players.

The first Houk team, the 1961 team, one of the greatest teams of all time, ran off 109 wins and finally shook a tough Detroit team in September to win the pennant. Houk had the horses and they were running – two of them chasing the great single-season home run record of Babe Ruth, the magic 60 set when the American League played 154 games. In 1961 the league expanded to 10 teams and a 162-game schedule, and maybe by coincidence, maybe not, 1961 was the season of the Mantle-Maris home run derby. Maris would break the record with

61 homers and Mantle would end up not far behind him with 54. Actually, a total of six 1961 Yankees hit 20 or more home runs: Maris, Mantle, Skowron (28), Berra (22), Elston Howard (21) and Johnny Blanchard (21). The team was so strong that Blanchard, a part-time catcher and outfielder who hit home runs in four consecutive at-bats at one point this year, had no regular position to call his own.

The 1961 Yankees also enjoyed outstanding fielding and pitching. They ranked a league first in fielding (.980), leading in double plays (180) and making the fewest errors (124). The Skowron-Richardson-Kubek-Boyer infield was the best in the game. Howard was playing well behind the plate, and in the outfield, Mantle was flanked by Maris, a great right fielder, and in left, by either Berra, who played a good outfield, or Hector Lopez, a fine hitter and a valuable fourth outfielder. Ford, with a 25-4 record and a new slider, led the pitching staff. He won the Cy Young Award, and, by winning 14 straight decisions, tied a Jack Chesbro club record set in 1904. Also part of this accomplished staff were Terry (16-3), Bill Stafford (14-9), Jim Coates (11-5) and Rollie Sheldon (11-5). Working out of the bullpen, Luis Arroyo (15-5) led the league in saves (29) and games pitched (65), his great screwball saving a peck of games for Whitey Ford.

But the main engine was the 115-homer performance of the M&M boys. Maris, the league's MVP for the second straight year, not only led the league in homers but in RBIs (142) and, in a tie with Mantle, in runs scored (132). Mantle hit .317 (compared with Maris' .269), and led the league in slugging (.687) and walks (126) besides his shared leadership in runs scored.

The Mantle-Maris rivalry was a friendly one. "I hope Roger hits 80 home runs," Mantle told a reporter, "and I hope I hit 81."

Maris had two advantages. For one, he had 76 more at-bats than did Mantle. For another, as the number three hitter, he had Mickey behind him in the order and pitchers were not likely to work around him to get to Mantle. Roger was not intentionally walked all season. Maris also enjoyed good health while Mantle in the season's final month was afflicted with a pulled muscle, a viral infection and an abscessed hip. For a good stretch of the 1961 season it

appeared that if anyone was to break the Ruth record it would be Mantle. The Mick did achieve one interesting statistic, a homer ratio of 10.5 per 100 at-bats. Only Ruth has ever enjoyed a better ratio than that. It is a ratio that suggests that Mantle, too, would have hit 61 homers – or perhaps 62 – had he as many at-bats as Maris.

But the brass ring went to Maris, who began his run after Ruth with a record-tying 15 homers in June. He put blips in his homer chart with four homers in a July doubleheader and seven during a six-game stretch in mid-August, and by September's start had a total of 51. His fifty-ninth, in the 154th game on September 20, led the Yankees to a 4-2 pennant-clinching win. His record-tying sixtieth was hit at Yankee Stadium on September 26. His sixty-first came on October 1, the last day of the season – 61 homers in the season of '61. Hit at Yankee Stadium off Boston's Tracy Stallard, the record-breaker was seen by a hard-to-believe turnout of only 23,154. Roger Maris, a small-town Midwesterner who didn't cotton to the tension of the big city, to begin with, and who was anything but enthralled with the attention and pressure generated by the chase, was relieved when it was over.

The Yankees won the 1961 World Series over Cincinnati in five games, making manager Houk only the third skipper in baseball history to win the game's greatest prize in his rookie season. Whitey Ford ran his string of scoreless innings in World Series competition to 32. Carrying over two

Above: *A ready and able Ralph Houk, who had undergone a bit of grooming for the manager's job, rides into the post after the calamity of the 1960 World Series. Assisted in no small way by the Mantle-Maris home run derby, Houk would win a World Championship in his first year as the Yanks' skipper.*

Above: *Roger Maris swings, and hits his 61st home run of the 1961 season on October 1, breaking Babe Ruth's record for most home runs in a single season.*

complete-game shutouts from the previous year's Series, Ford this year added a two-hit shutout in game one and five innings of shutout baseball in game four before a foot injury forced his departure. His new World Series record broke Ruth's mark of 29 and two-thirds scoreless innings, a record the slugger had treasured. And Whitey would run the record to 33 and two-thirds innings in the 1962 World Series.

Ford in 1962 won 17 games, but the club's big winner, with 23 wins, was Ralph Terry. For Terry, who had all the basic pitches and mixed them well, it was the crowning season of his career.

The M&M boys' homer production, quite naturally, fell from the stratosphere in 1962. Maris hit 33 and Mantle 30. Maris saw fewer good pitches and in one game was intentionally walked four times. However, the M&M boys were handsomely complemented by Skowron (23 homers, 80 RBIs), Howard (21 homers, 91 RBIs) and Rookie-of-the-Year Tom Tresh (20 homers, 93 RBIs). Filling in for Kubek at shortstop while Tony served with the military, the switch-hitting Tresh was the first of several young players to evoke "Mantle expecta-

tions." Mantle, meanwhile, was winning the league MVP Award for the third and final time. The Mick hit .321 and led the league in slugging (.605) and walks (122). He also won a Gold Glove, and he did all this in spite of injuries that forced him to miss many games and to play hurt when he did take the field. His body was battered and bruised but his spirit was now in the tender care of peer admiration and public adulation.

No one was more victimized by "Mantle expectations" than was Mickey Mantle. He could never do enough. After a 1958 season in which he hit 42 homers and batted .304, Casey Stengel said of his star: "I never saw a ballplayer who had greater promise. He could be the best there ever was. . . . Every year he ought to lead the league in everything. Nobody hits the ball farther, right- or left-handed. Nobody is faster running to first base, or stealing. . . . There isn't anything wrong with his arm, and he can catch anything out there, except when he gets careless, which he does when he starts thinking about the foreign situation, the national debt and maybe his putting."

In 1960 things changed. Instead of

demanding more from Mickey, the press and public placed a few demands on themselves; they made themselves take a fairer look at Mickey and they discovered a gritty, determined competitor who played the game to win. Almost overnight there was an en masse perceptual swing; Mickey in the 1960s became as loved and cheered as he was criticized and booed in the 1950s.

But Ole Case had it right when he said, "Nobody hits the ball farther." Mickey would come close to hitting one clear out of Yankee Stadium, something that has never been done. On May 22, 1963, he belted one off Kansas City's Bill Fischer that hit near the top of the old green facade in right field. He had done that several times before, but this time the ball was still rising when it met the copper decoration. How far might it have gone unobstructed? A minimum of 620 feet, a physicist estimated. Years earlier, after Mantle hit a measured 565-footer in Washington, the great Bob Feller was quoted as saying, "There isn't a man that ever played baseball who could hit a ball 600 feet under his own power." But Mantle hit one in Detroit on September 10, 1960, that was measured trigonometrically in 1985 as having traveled 643 feet. While measurements are not always reliable in terms of either the procedure or impact point used, there is little doubt that Mantle's power was beyond the extraordinary.

The Yankees won their twentieth World Championship by beating San Francisco in a rain-harassed 1962 World Series that dragged over 13 days. The hero: the man who served the Mazeroski homer in 1960, Ralph Terry, who this time around won two games, including a dramatic 1-0 decision in game seven.

Ralph Houk would manage again in 1963 and win one more pennant before passing the reins to Yogi Berra who, at 38, served as a player-coach and caught in 35 games. Elston Howard was now the regular catcher, the league's best catcher, and not only that, but the league's MVP. He won a Gold Glove for his catching, hit .287 with 28 homers and, with Mantle and Maris hurt much of the year, functioned as the Yankees' big gun. The Berra-to-Howard transition was a smooth one. A versatile ballplayer, Howard in his early Yankee career worked in the outfield and at first base in addition to serving behind the plate. Progressively, he played more and caught more until, by 1960, he was the regular catcher at the age of 31. His easy-going manner off the field and competitive nature on it were welcomed attributes.

The team was slowly changing. A new regular in 1963, first baseman Joe Pepitone (27 homers, 89 RBIs) proved to be up to the challenge of replacing the traded Skowron. Ford had his best year (24-7, 2.74 ERA) and a newcomer in the rotation, Jim Bouton (21-7, 2.53 ERA), was a breath of fresh air. Bouton was part of a new wave of irreverent Yankees, which included Pepitone and back-up infielder Phil Linz. He was his own man who didn't buy into many of the ballplayer and club attitudes. He was open with the press and his reading went beyond *The Sporting News*. The other players didn't know quite what to make of him, but he was a bulldog on the mound, and they liked that.

The 1963 Yankees had a tremendous defensive infield. Richardson won a Gold Glove at second base and many baseball observers regarded Boyer as the best-fielding third sacker ever. Pepitone was lithe, quick and agile at first, and the consistent Kubek was the glue at shortstop.

But a good defense will not beat a Sandy Koufax. The Los Angeles Dodgers' ace fanned 15 Yankees while beating them in game one of the 1963 World Series, 5-2, then returned to whip them again in game four, 2-1. With in-between victories by Johnny Podres and Don Drysdale, the Dodgers gained the World Championship in the minimum four games. It was the first crack in the Yankees' Dynasty.

The Yankees looked ahead to a new year and a new manager, the one and only Yogi Berra. But the results in 1964 would be the same, another pennant, although this time in a difficult race with Chicago and Baltimore – the crack was widening – and

Below: *That cute little left-hander, Whitey Ford, winner of 236 regular-season games for the Yankees, plus another 22 in World Series play.*

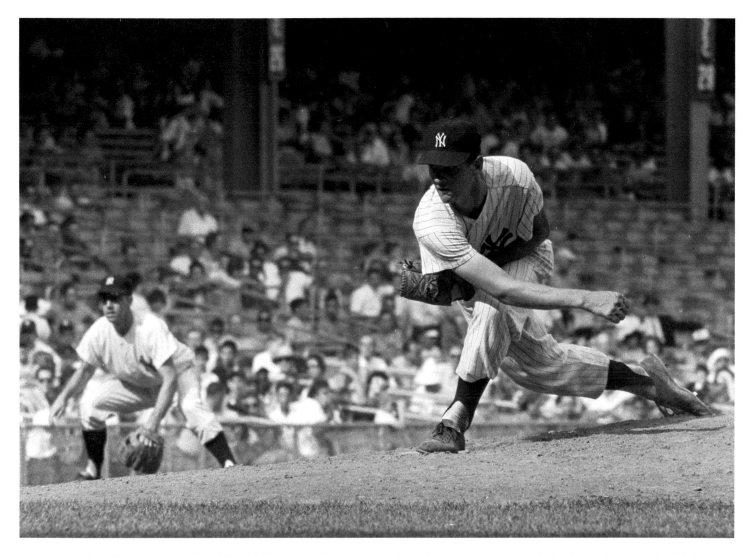

Above: *Ralph Terry brings it home. The server of the home run that sank the Yankees in the 1960 World Series proved the pitching hero in the conquest of the San Francisco Giants in the 1962 Series. Clete Boyer guards at third.*

Opposite above: *Bobby Richardson wings the ball to first as San Francisco's Orlando Cepeda crashes into second base with spikes high in the 1962 World Series.*

Opposite below: *Tim McCarver, front man in a double steal, reaches home safely for St. Louis in the seventh game of the 1964 World Series, won by St. Louis. The catcher is Elston Howard.*

another World Series defeat. It was also the last great season for Mickey Mantle (35 homers, 111 RBIs, .303 batting average). The Yankees were forced to concede the World Championship to the St. Louis Cardinals in a tough seven-game struggle. They were up against another great pitcher, hard-throwing Bob Gibson, who twice had complete-game victories in which he struck out 13 and nine.

The Cardinals were managed by Johnny Keane who, like Joe McCarthy, never played in the majors but who won the admiration of Ralph Houk, now New York's general manager. Keane resigned the day after the Series ended, a day on which Berra was fired. Then Keane became the Yankees' manager. He inherited a team that had lost its way, as subsequent events would show. Owners Del Webb, absorbed in the construction business, and Dan Topping, who was not enjoying the best of health, decided in 1962 to unload the club, and until they found a buyer, they also decided they would make only urgent expenditures. The franchise suffered accordingly over the couple of years before the sale transpired. That was on November 12, 1964, and the buyer was CBS, the broadcasting giant putting down $11.2 million for

80 percent of the franchise and picking up the other 20 percent later.

The farm system had run dry, and in June of 1965, the first annual amateur free agent draft – an attempt to break up the Yankees – was held. The Yankees' advantage in signing top high school and college prospects, which depended on a highly developed scouting system, was brought to an end. The few people in baseball to oppose the draft were those connected with top-flight organizations like the Yankees. So Keane was coming to New York at the wrong time. On top of this, he was the wrong man. He made a poor match with both the club and the City of New York. In his first year of 1965 the Yankees finished a dismal sixth; the crack in the Yankees Dynasty had become a gaping rift.

The 1964 World Series appearance of the Yankees would be their last until 1976. Yankees fans would have to live with memories. One that many doubtless cherished was a home run at Yankee Stadium in game three of that Series. With the score 1-1 in the ninth, an ailing Mickey Mantle blasted one into the upper deck in right field to give New York the win and set off unrestrained joy in the Bronx. Trouble was, nobody thought to bottle it.

6. Long Years of Denial

Everyone somewhere along the line – in junior high, high school, college – has rooted for a loser, even has become used to pulling for the Poor Wildcats or Poor Whatever. But Yankees fans, sent reeling by their club's sixth-place finish in 1965, didn't take easily to losing; they had become accustomed to winning, and they expected 1966 would right a world turned upside down. Yet 1966 would deal the cruelest blow of all – a tenth-place finish. Tenth place in a 10-team league! Keane was dismissed as Yankees manager with the team at 4-16, and only eight months after leaving the job made so gleamingly attractive by Huggins, McCarthy and Stengel, Johnny Keane, who had a heart condition, was dead.

The 1966 Yankees had some power, with Joe Pepitone, Tom Tresh and Mickey Mantle putting together 81 home runs, but the team hit only .235, and its pitching staff was mediocre. Still, these Yankees, managed by Ralph Houk who came down from the front office, were not as inept as their league standing might suggest. They had the best winning percentage (.440, 70-89) of any last-place team in league history.

But no mistake about it, the Dark Ages

had descended on a team grown old. Tony Kubek had already retired. Mantle was winding down and Bobby Richardson and Hector Lopez would retire with the close of the season. The once-feared Roger Maris and the slick-fielding Clete Boyer would be dealt away, unprofitably. Ellie Howard would be traded and Whitey Ford would retire in 1967. The Yankees needed good young players, but the farm system was dry. Gloom, gloom and more gloom. The season of disenchantment, when on one September day only 413 fans bothered to go to Yankee Stadium to watch the once-proud New Yorkers bow to Chicago, 4-1. Home attendance fell to 1,124,648, the lowest since 1945.

The Dark Ages continued through 1967 with its ninth-place finish. Mantle was almost the whole show. Amid the gloom, Mickey hit his 500th career homer on May 13 off Baltimore's Stu Miller at Yankee Stadium. It won the game, which was the important thing to Mantle. Mickey, however, no longer resembled the Mick of old. His knees were nearly shot and he played first base to ease the pain.

Mantle had entered the majors with osteomyelitis, and health maintenance never got easier for him. Knee injuries forced three operations, two on the right knee and one on the left. He developed arthritis in his right knee, suffered ligament and cartilage damage in both knees – he had little or no cartilage left in either knee – and sustained countless pulled and torn leg muscles. An injury he sustained in 1957 to his right shoulder never really healed and he reinjured the shoulder in 1965, further handicapping his throwing and left-handed hitting. But there never was a more determined ballplayer; he suited up and played more games (2401) than anyone in Yankees history.

The 1968 Yankees climbed to fifth place, but in 1969 the season opened on a subdued note with Mantle missing from the Yankees dugout, the Mick having announced his retirement at spring training camp in Fort Lauderdale. However drab, the Mantleless Yankees of 1969

Below: *With his great stroke for Yankee Stadium, left-handed Joe Pepitone takes a cut on April 10, 1962. He would be one of the Yanks' few bright spots in the otherwise-gloomy mid-1960s.*

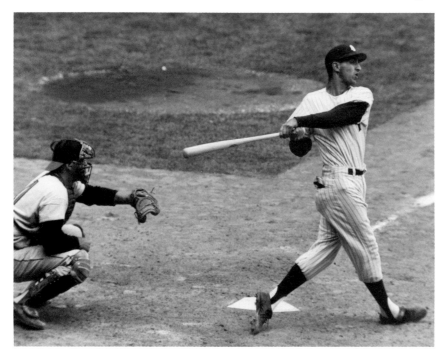

couldn't finish any worse than sixth; for the first time in history, the major leagues were divided into divisions and six teams were assigned to the East Division of the American League. The Yankees, who managed to finish fifth, had only two power hitters, Joe Pepitone (27 homers, 70 RBIs) and Bobby Murcer (26 homers, 82 RBIs), and Pepitone would be traded two months after the curtain fell on the season.

Pepitone was more than a three-time Gold Glove first baseman and a fine left-handed hitter with a natural home run stroke for Yankee Stadium; he was a personality. The colorful Brooklynite drew supporters and antagonists all around the league. He was long-haired and loose in an era when young people were loosening up. He was fun and he sought fun, to the point, some might say, where he sacrificed the chance to become one of baseball's all-time greats.

With "Pepi" gone, the 1970 Yankees were virtually colorless – but not without interest. The club won 93 games, going way beyond expectations, and finished second, although 15 games behind powerful Baltimore. The year might have been Ralph Houk's best and was a credit to the trio running the pinstriped show: Houk, the field manager, Lee MacPhail, the general manager, and the club president, Michael Burke.

Son of Larry MacPhail and an astute baseball executive in his own right, Lee MacPhail had worked under George Weiss with the Yankees and later helped build the Orioles into a successful franchise. Lee was as mild-mannered and reserved as his father was bombastic. Burke, a CBS executive, became Yankees president in 1966. To restore the Yankees to their former luster required more money than CBS was ready to invest, yet Burke, with MacPhail and Houk, held things together and now, finally, in 1970, they had a second-place finish.

Burke, to his lasting credit, kept the Yankees in Yankee Stadium. New Jersey officials were aggressively boring into the Big Apple, enticing its teams to cross the Hudson. The football Giants crossed, but not the Yankees. Burke, instead, promoted the renovation of Yankee Stadium, and the Yankees would, in 1972, sign a 30-year lease to play in a remodeled Yankee Stadium, and in 1987 they would extend this commitment to 2032.

The leaders of the 1970 Yankees' offense were Roy White (22 homers, 94 RBIs, .296 batting average) and Bobby Murcer (23 homers, 78 RBIs). White, a soft-spoken, intelligent Californian, brought the club a touch of class, and he would be a Yankee

from 1965 through 1979. Besides being a good, slashing line-drive hitter, he had an ability to draw walks and steal bases. He was also a fine left fielder, although he lacked a strong throwing arm.

Twenty-four-year-old Bobby Murcer, the new idol of Yankees fans, had the misfortune of being compared with Mantle. He and Mantle were from Oklahoma, both were signed by scout Tom Greenwade, both began as shortstops before becoming center fielders, and both reached the majors at age 19. Bobby was an excellent all-around player, one of baseball's best over the 1971-73 seasons. He would lead the Yankees in RBIs six straight seasons. He was the new Big Guy, the star, but he was no Mantle.

The 1970 Yankees also had the league's Rookie of the Year – Thurman Munson. Thurman was already regarded as an outstanding defensive catcher and his .302 batting average was considered a nice bonus. This was a guy the Yankees could build around. Munson had starred at Kent State in Ohio and was scouted by former Yankee Gene Woodling, who advised the Yankees to "GET HIM." The Yanks' first selection in the 1968 draft, he signed for a $75,000 bonus and now, after fewer than 100 games in the minors, was already the Yankees' cornerstone.

The Yankees in 1970 had three strong hurlers in Mel Stottlemyre, Fritz Peterson and Stan Bahnsen. Stottlemyre, a 15-game

Above: *Thurman Munson, Rookie of the Year in 1970, was an outstanding catcher and reliable hitter for the Yankees until his tragic death in 1979.*

Right: In his seven-year Yankee career, 1972-78, reliever Sparky Lyle saved 141 games and won 57.

and finished only six points behind the batting champ, Tony Oliva. White (19 homers, 84 RBIs, .292 batting average) played 145 games without making an error.

The Yankees in March 1972 further strengthened their solidifying nucleus by making a great trade with Boston. For Danny Cater and Mario Guerrero, they landed the one and only Albert Walter Lyle, better known as "Sparky." A left-handed reliever with a biting slider, Lyle was an immediate Yankees star in 1972, saving 35 games. He seemed to be almost single-handedly keeping the Yankees in the pennant race through the first weeks of September. Although the Yankees placed fourth, they were only six and a half out at the finish.

The trade for Lyle was the first in a series of great trades in the 1970s. It was Lee Mac-Phail who obtained Lyle and who in November 1972 made the trade that brought Graig Nettles from Cleveland. The next Yankees regime, under George Steinbrenner, would deal for Lou Piniella, Chris Chambliss and Dick Tidrow (1974); Oscar Gamble, Mickey Rivers, Ed Figueroa, Willie Randolph and Dock Ellis (1976); and Paul Blair, Bucky Dent, Mike Torrez and Cliff Johnson (1977).

But Lyle and the 1972 pennant race notwithstanding, it was hard to believe in a club so lacking in offense. Except for Murcer (33 homers, 96 RBIs, .292 batting average), the Bombers weren't bombing and the fans weren't coming. Attendance figures in 1972 dipped below one million. CBS wasn't happy and Mike Burke was told to either buy the club or get it sold.

It was the general manager of the Cleveland Indians, Gabe Paul, who brought Burke and a Clevelander named George Steinbrenner together. Burke and Steinbrenner formed a group that on January 3, 1973, reportedly for between $10 and $12 million, bought the Yankees. Burke would be eased out of the picture, stepping down as president in April and remaining one of Steinbrenner's limited partners. MacPhail and Houk would soon leave, too, and Paul would move over to the Yankees, becoming president. The Steinbrenner stewardship was off and running.

Steinbrenner wanted success. Yet in the common meaning of the term, he was not as a young man success-driven. Unlike so many young people on today's college campuses, he did not set out to amass a fortune. He was an English major. He ran low hurdles and played halfback on the Williams College football team, and after graduation he taught and coached. He became an assistant football coach at Northwestern University and later at Purdue. He

winner, had been called up from Richmond in the heat of the 1964 pennant race and posted a 9-3 record, rescuing the pennant for the Yankees. Had Mel's career not coincided with New York's decline, he might today rank among the greatest of Yankees hurlers. The sinkerball artist from Hazelton, Missouri, won at least 20 games for three mediocre Yankees teams and was selected for five All-Star Games.

Peterson, too, had the misfortune of pitching for the Yankees at the wrong time. He was a left-handed control pitcher who had his best season in 1970, going 20-11 and walking only 40 batters in 260 innings pitched. A little flaky and a practical joker, he was serious all the same when he and teammate Mike Kekich announced in 1973 that they had exchanged families – wives, kids, pets and all. Bahnsen, the 1968 Rookie of the Year, won 14 games in 1970. He would be traded in December 1971 to Chicago, and in his first season there won 21 games.

But things were looking up for the Yankees. A certain chemistry was coming together, even though there was still a way to go, the club slipping to fourth in 1971. Murcer and White once more were productive. Murcer (25 homers, 94 RBIs, .331 batting average) came into his own at the plate didn't go running off to the family business, a Great Lakes ore-hauling fleet called Kinsman Transit. It was the business, having fallen on hard times, that came after him. George helped his late father put the firm back on a money-making track and later, with others, bought the American Ship Building Company. Along the way he also dabbled in various show business and sports enterprises.

As a boy in Cleveland, George had been a card-carrying member of the Yankees Haters International. Still, the Yankees gave him a special thrill when they came to town, and when in 1973 he and his co-investors had the chance to buy the storied club, he likened it to a chance to buy the Mona Lisa.

In 1973, Houk's last year as manager, the Yankees finished an unsatisfying fourth in spite of Munson's emergence as a complete hitter (20 homers, .301 batting average) and fine seasons from Murcer (22 homers, 95 RBIs, .304 batting average) and Graig Nettles (22 homers, 81 RBIs).

This season spelled the birth of the American League's designated hitter rule, and the first Yankees DH was Ron Blomberg. Blomberg, one of the Yankees' top prospects in the late 1960s, possessed a booming left-handed stroke, and as a Jewish lad from Georgia, he had a big following in New York's large Jewish community. It looked like he would finally emerge as a star in 1973, when he had his batting average above the .400 mark in early July and finished at .329. Thereafter, however, his career was sabotaged by a succession of injuries and an inability to handle left-handed pitching.

The dismantling of the grand old lady of baseball, old Yankee Stadium, began in 1973. The last game at the old Stadium was played September 30, and many in the crowd left with momentos of America's most famous sports venue. The remodeling of the Stadium was to include the replacing of columns with a column-free, cantilevered support system. While the work was underway, the Yankees in 1974 and 1975 would play at Shea Stadium, home of the Mets.

The Yankees, meanwhile, were searching for a new manager. Dick Williams, manager of the World Champion Oakland A's, resigned after the 1973 World Series and was hired by the Yankees, only to have Charlie Finley, the A's owner, argue that Williams was still bound to the A's. Finley was upheld by Joe Cronin, president of the American League, and the Yankees were left without a skipper. They turned, then, to Bill Virdon, former National League outfielder.

Finishing only two games out, the Yankees in 1974 came as close to a title as they had in a decade. In early September they surged past fading Boston and held on to first place until Baltimore took it from them with a three-game sweep at Shea Stadium in mid-September. The Orioles made it difficult for the Yankees to overtake them, winning 28 of their last 34 games. Still, Virdon's men were after the Birds right up to that final weekend of the season when Murcer suffered a damaged thumb trying to break up a fight and had to be sidelined. It turned out that the very hit that eliminated the Yankees from contention might have been an out had Bobby been playing his position. Murcer was a right fielder now, Virdon having inserted the gifted Elliott Maddox into center in one of his gutsier moves.

The Yanks' top four RBI men were Murcer, with 88; Nettles, 75; Piniella, 70; and Munson, 60. The club needed a *big* RBI man, preferably a right-handed power hitter because the Yankees were overloaded with lefty sticks. So a few weeks after the close of the 1974 season Gabe Paul made a bold, stunning trade. He sent Murcer, the

Below: *Bobby Murcer, a solid hitter, finished second in the batting race in 1971 with a .331 average. He went to the Giants in 1974 in exchange for Bobby Bonds.*

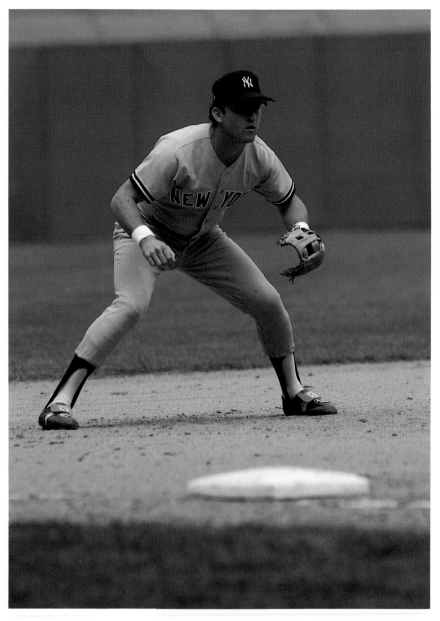

Above: *Outstanding as a defensive third sacker, Graig Nettles could also hit with power. He is sixth on the all-time Yankee home run list.*

Right: *The "Catfish," Jim Hunter. He won 63 games for the Yankees in five campaigns.*

fans' favorite, to the San Francisco Giants for Bobby Bonds, a talented right-handed hitter. Bonds was powerful, fast and strong-armed. He was also, however, a strikeout king and a Californian with a California lifestyle. New York City would not be Bonds' cup of tea.

Gabe Paul had better success with a pair of trades he had engineered several months earlier. In December 1973 he sent Lindy McDaniel, once the ace of the Yankees' bullpen, and another pitcher to the Kansas City Royals for outfielder Lou Piniella. Lou hit .305 for New York in 1974 and added to the growing nucleus of solid players. In April 1974 Paul sent four pitchers – almost half his staff – to Cleveland for three players, including first baseman Chris Chambliss and pitcher Dick Tidrow. Chambliss got off to a slow start in 1974 but would improve rapidly, and Tidrow was to prove a valuable addition in several mound roles.

The fans found the 1974 Yankees interesting. One focus of attraction was Graig Nettles, who with the fading of Baltimore's Brooks Robinson was becoming the league's premier defensive third baseman. Nettles had the ability to position himself far from the line and yet spear hot shots down the line, seeing the ball into his glove with his body parallel to the ground, then springing up and firing to nail a base-runner. He was a productive hitter, but he was most winsome in the field, a real treat for Yankees fans who had not seen able, let alone spectacular, play at the hot corner since Clete Boyer's departure following the 1966 season.

These 1974 Yankees, in spite of the formidable play of Baltimore, might have taken the division title had Stottlemyre stayed well. Mel suffered a shoulder injury in mid-season, and at the age of 32, was forced to give up the game. Stottlemyre might have added just enough talent and experience to an already fine pitching staff, led by Pat Dobson and Doc Medich – both 19-15 – to pull it off for New York.

The Yankees were not about to come up short in 1975: A line was cast for the great Catfish Hunter, who was declared a free agent when Oakland owner Charlie Finley failed to meet certain terms of Hunter's contract. On New Year's Eve, as 1974 became 1975, Catfish became a Yankee, signing a five-year contract, a complicated package said to be worth $3.25 million. The results of the arbitrated Hunter case, and those of other cases even more basic to baseball's precious reserve clause that bound a player, essentially, to his club for life, were breaking down an old system; players were gaining more control over their careers. "Free agent," the short name for all of this, produced opportunities that George Steinbrenner didn't necessarily welcome but did elect to exploit. Naturally, the Yankees in time would be accused of "buying" success.

Whatever they were buying, it was not success in 1975, despite having Bonds (32 homers, 85 RBIs, 30 stolen bases) and Catfish (23-14, 2.58 ERA). They fell to third in the standings, a fat dozen games behind the division-winning Red Sox. When the club's record was 53-51, Virdon was fired and Billy Martin was hired as manager.

On the surface, Bonds had a great year. He was the first Yankee ever to hit 30 homers and steal 30 bases, even while hampered by leg and knee injuries much of the season. But he wasn't the big run producer the Yankees needed. The Yankees weren't sure if he was a lead-off man or a third-place hitter, and so, after only a single year in pinstripes, Bonds would go to the California Angels for Mickey Rivers, an outfielder, and Ed Figueroa, a pitcher.

Munson was actually the Yankees' best player in 1975. He hit .318, his career high, drove in 102 runs, and collected his third straight Gold Glove for his fielding. He was a tenacious catcher, with a quick-release throw that gave the willies to thieving baserunners. He wouldn't back down from home plate collisions, which were becoming increasingly worrisome because of his offensive indispensability. He was the team leader, offensively, in the field, and in the clubhouse. In 1976 he would be named captain – the first Yankees captain since no less than Lou Gehrig.

And yet the real star of the 1975 Yankees was Billy Martin. The igniter of the 1950s Yankees, the brawler, the Brat, Casey's boy, was back. The Yankees finished 1975 going 30-26 under Martin, not a whole lot better than under Virdon. But Billy was back, and in a job he had dreamed about, and a certain promise was there.

Billy, as a player, had taken his exile from New York hard. He was unfairly blamed for the 1957 Copa mess, although he would, in his lifetime, show such a propensity for Copa-like incidents as to tax the limits of human understanding. He had bounced around in baseball for a half-dozen years and finished his playing career with Minnesota in 1961. He then worked his way up to become the Twins' skipper in 1969. In his first year he led the Twins to an AL West title. He was next with Detroit, leading the Tigers to an AL East title in 1972. Then it was on to Texas where in 1974 he brought the hapless Rangers up to a second-place finish. But he seemed to always have trouble with the front office.

His return to New York was widely applauded. Billy was back, and with many fans, that was all that mattered. If anyone could turn things around for the Yankees it was Billy Martin. At long last, a *winner* was in charge.

Billy and the Yankees didn't do it in 1975. But they had the makings, and next year they would be at home in their gleaming new digs in the Bronx. A feeling was growing that the Yankees and their fans were about to be delivered from the Dark Ages.

Below: *Manager Billy Martin in his in-your-face posture as he tries to make a point with umpire Drew Coble.*

7. Feasting After the Famine

It was a delicious year, 1976. The nation was celebrating the bicentennial of its Declaration of Independence and on top of this Yankees fans could welcome an attractive team to an attractive new home. Renovated Yankee Stadium had the old Stadium's basic geometry as well as a concrete replica of its distinguishing copper facade. So while spanking new, it remained connected with its glorious past.

Could life for Yankees adherents possibly get any better? Would Billy Martin do as well managing in New York as he had in three other cities? He would. Would he do well enough to lead the Yankees to their first pennant in a dozen years? He would.

His team was balanced. It had a couple of speedsters in Mickey Rivers and Willie Randolph and a slew of excellent heads-up baserunners, and Martin employed an aggressive running game. It was powered by Graig Nettles, the league leader with 32 homers, and Thurman Munson, Chris Chambliss and new Yankee Oscar Gamble who each popped 17. It also had good fielding and good pitching. Its big winner was Ed Figueroa (19-10, 3.02 ERA), and while Catfish Hunter, his best days now behind him, slipped to 17-15, Hunter was helping the Yankees learn how to win, and in the league playoffs would pitch a neat five-hitter. Sparky Lyle and Dick Tidrow anchored a solid bullpen.

A few off-season trades made the 1976 Yankees click so well they finished 10 and a half games ahead of the field. Gamble, ob-

Right: *Like Earle Combs and Roy White, outfielder Mickey Rivers did not have a rifle of an arm, but he was lightning-quick, both in the field and on the bases.*

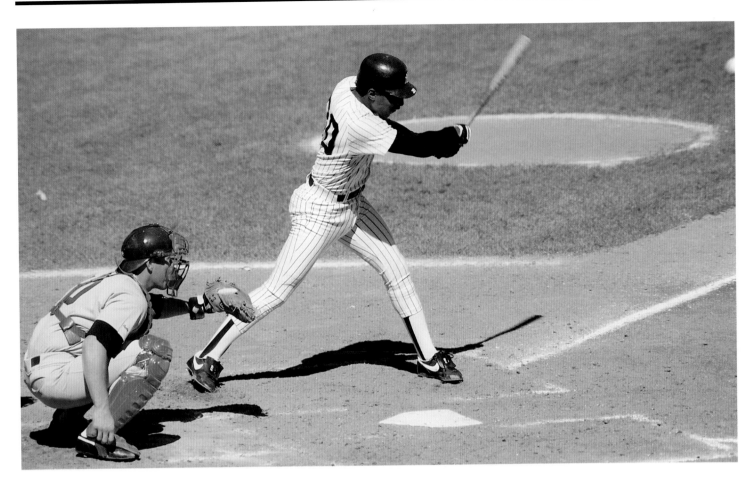

tained from Cleveland, provided good left-handed power. Second baseman Randolph and pitcher Dock Ellis (17-8, 3.19 ERA) came from Pittsburgh for Doc Medich, a reliable but unspectacular pitcher. Randolph not only added speed but the quality of his play at second base was unseen around the Bronx since the days of Bobby Richardson. And the Bobby Bonds-for-Figueroa-and-Rivers deal netted the pitching staff's biggest winner – Figueroa – and a ground-covering center fielder – Rivers – who hit .312, scored 95 runs, and accounted for 43 of the Bronx Bandits' 163 stolen bases.

The Yankees were already set behind the plate with Thurman Munson, the team's leader and the league's 1976 MVP. Munson hit .302 with 105 RBIs and handled the pitching staff skillfully. A clutch player, he would hit .435 in the upcoming League Championship Series, and .529 in the World Series.

New York and Kansas City seesawed back and forth in the 1976 Championship Series to force a fifth, deciding game. The Yankees were winning until George Brett hit a three-run eighth-inning homer to tie the score, 6-6. Leading off the bottom of the ninth, Chris Chambliss, a .524 hitter in the Series, put a Mark Littell pitch over the right-field wall and the Yankee Stadium crowd of nearly 57,000 erupted onto the field in such frenzied celebration that Chambliss was barely able to make it home to touch the plate.

With their thirtieth league pennant, the Yankees won the dubious right to meet Cincinnati – the awesome Big Red Machine – in the World Series. They could do little more than watch the loaded Reds – Rose, Morgan, Bench, Foster, Griffey, Gullett, Nolan, and more – walk away with the World Championship in four games.

Next year would be different. The Yankees would have a new guy. Reggie Jackson played out his option with Baltimore and on November 29, 1976, signed with the Yankees for about $3 million. Jackson was the biggest name in baseball, having, prior to his one year in Baltimore, played nine seasons with the A's. He hit 47 homers in 1969, was the league's MVP in 1973 and led Oakland to three World Championships. He was recognized as a winner, a clutch performer and a drawing card.

Jackson became a Yankee by becoming part of the first free agent re-entry draft. He was free to refuse to sign with Baltimore because baseball's ancient reserve clause, which bound a player to his club, was stricken down by the courts in 1976. A ballplayer who had satisfied his contract and who had six years in the "show" could take his services elsewhere. That's how the Yankees got Jackson to ink a five-year contract, and how they got pitcher Don Gullett, another multimillion-dollar acquisition.

George Steinbrenner, the Yankees' principal owner, said he had no special liking

Above: *Steady Willie Randolph normally hit between .270 and .300 in 13 years as a Yankee.*

Right: *A force to be reckoned with – the articulate and, at times, poetic Reggie Jackson. Reggie will long be remembered for his three home runs in the final game of the 1977 World Series.*

Right: *Reggie and manager Billy Martin (left) almost came to televised blows in a 1977 game in Boston when Martin lifted Reggie in mid-inning after what seemed like a casual play on a bloop double by Jim Rice.*

for free agency. Nor did the fans, particularly. Free agency was making instant millionaires of dozens of players – even mediocre players were getting rich. Millionaire movie stars, stock jockeys or makers of adulterated orange juice were okay, but making a million for playing a boy's game? The fans and Steinbrenner alike have trouble with that one. In the last analysis, it was with the owners that the power to prevent a runaway players' market lay. They could show restraint, a course Steinbrenner was later to follow, thus serving their own good interests and possibly the interests of the fans as well. But there was no restraining Steinbrenner in the late 1970s. George got the best of the free agents. He was willing to plunk down millions, as signaled by his signing of Hunter, and he got his money's worth. His 1976 signing of Jackson drove home his determination to build a new Yankees Dynasty.

With Jackson wearing pinstripes in 1977, emotions ran high. Baseball addicts in cities whose clubs refrained from entering the free agent market resented the new system. They regarded Reggie as an overpaid opportunist and feared another period of domination by the Yankees, all on the strength of the purse.

Reggie personally added to the controversy in 1977. True, he wasn't particularly welcomed by his new teammates, who felt they had done fine without him in 1976. And true, Billy Martin resented the chumminess that existed between Reggie and Steinbrenner. But Reggie added to the hard feelings when he strutted into spring training and announced: "I think Reggie Jackson on your ball club is a part of a show of force. It's a show of power. I help to intimidate the opposition, just because I'm here." His new teammates rolled their eyes.

It was during spring camp that Reggie made careless remarks to a *Sport* magazine writer. When the story hit the stands in May, Munson became furious and carried around a copy of the magazine. "I'm the straw that stirs the drink," the story quoted Reggie as saying. "It all comes back to me. Maybe I should say me and Munson but really he doesn't enter into it. . . . Munson thinks he can be the straw that stirs the drink but he can only stir it bad."

With these remarks, Reggie had effectively broken off relations with Munson and further alienated the team. Then, in a June game in Boston, Reggie and his manager almost exchanged nationally televised punches in the dugout. The decorum-minded Joe McCarthy, winding down a long life on his farm in upstate New York, must have wondered what the hell was going on. Martin thought Reggie had dogged it in going after a ball, and in the middle of the inning he sent Paul Blair in to replace Jackson. Reggie returned to the dugout and the blows nearly came when Reggie, according to Martin, swore at him. According to Jackson, it was Martin who did the first swearing – and threatening. Meanwhile, the Red Sox were hardly easing tensions in launching 16 homers in their three-game sweep of the Yankees.

But New York's hardened professionals refused to come unglued. They played a little better than .500 ball until early August when they began playing .800 ball, ending up with a 100-62 record. The closest competition, Baltimore and Boston, were both two and a half games behind at the end. The potent bats: Jackson (32 homers, 110 RBIs, .286 batting average), Nettles (37 homers, 107 RBIs), Munson (18 homers, 100 RBIs, .308 batting average), Chambliss (17 homers, 90 RBIs, .287 batting average), Lou Piniella (12 homers, .330 batting average), Rivers (12 homers, .326 batting average) and Roy White (14 homers, .268 batting average). A mid-season deal with Houston added Cliff Johnson (12 homers, .296 batting average) to the firepower.

The indispensable Sparky Lyle saved 26 games and won another 13, becoming the first relief pitcher in league history to win the Cy Young Award. Lyle would be traded after a 1978 season in which he played in the shadow of Goose Gossage, triggering Nettles' observation: "In one year Sparky has gone from Cy Young to sayonara." Great as Lyle was, it was Ron Guidry, who joined the rotation in June and who recorded most of his wins down the pennant

Below: One of the great Yankee stars of the 1970s and 1980s, Ron Guidry. Guidry, who had three 20-plus-win seasons, retired in 1989.

stretch, who turned it around for the Yankees in 1977. Guidry and Figueroa won a team-high 16 games each and Don Gullett and Mike Torrez each won 14 games. The pitchers were supported by probably the best defensive infield in baseball, with Gold Glover Nettles at third, steady Bucky Dent at shortstop, the excellent Willie Randolph at second and the throw-saving Chambliss at first.

Again it was Kansas City in the League Championship Series. The Royals took a two-games-to-one lead as the Series shifted to Kansas City, but Lyle in game four pitched five and a third innings of scoreless relief, winning and setting the stage for the decider. Jackson wasn't in the starting lineup for the finale. ("We need to talk," catcher Fran Healy told him before the game. "You're not playing.") But in the eighth inning, with the Royals ahead, 3-1, Reggie came to the plate as a pinch hitter and singled home a run, cutting it to 3-2. Paul Blair, playing for Jackson, singled in

Right: *He would sometimes seem intrigued by things no more exotic than a moth. Here Reginald Martinez Jackson ponders the path of a foul ball.*

the ninth. White followed with a walk and Rivers singled to tie the score. A Randolph sacrifice fly and an error gave New York a 5-3 advantage, which Lyle made stand up. Time now for the benchwarmer to become Mr. October.

The Yankees won the World Series by defeating Los Angeles in six games. It was a wild night at Yankee Stadium for game six, the crowd anticipating the first Yankees' World Championship since 1962, and the Dodgers jumping out to a 2-0 first-inning lead. Jackson walked in the second inning and Chambliss homered to draw the Yankees even, only to have Los Angeles take the lead, 3-2. Reggie homered in the fourth and again in the fifth, and in the eighth, he launched a ball that landed in the center-field bleachers more than 450 feet from home plate. Jackson's three-homer game led the Yankees to a convincing 8-4 victory and their first World Championship in 15 years.

Reggie Jackson, benched except for one at-bat in the vital final game with Kansas City, was the star of the final game of the World Series. He was Mr. October, having for the Series: a record five home runs, a record 10 runs, a record 25 total bases, and a .450 batting average. His was one of the great performances in World Series history.

As 1977 ended happily, 1978 began miserably. Injuries decimated the Yankees, and controversies popped up almost daily. Boston was pulling away from the field and was loaded with mauling sluggers – Jim Rice, Dwight Evans, Fred Lynn, Carlton Fisk, Carl Yastrzemski, Butch Hobson and George Scott. The Yanks had their work cut out for them. Then on July 17, in the bottom of the tenth inning against the Royals, Jackson struck out attempting a sacrifice bunt even after Martin ordered him to hit away. The Yankees lost in 11 innings and would soon be 14 games behind Boston.

The insubordinate Jackson was suspended for five days, and after rejoining the team, which was doing well without him, he found himself riding the bench. Then it happened. A still-stewing Martin would try to get two birds with one stone. "One's a born liar," he told reporters, "and the other's convicted."

The "one" was Jackson; the "other" was Steinbrenner, who had made illegal political contributions to Richard Nixon in 1974, a felony for which he has since been pardoned (by Ronald Reagan). The next day, July 24, Martin, under heat, resigned and was replaced by Bob Lemon. And then, only five days later, it was dramatically announced on Old Timers' Day that Martin

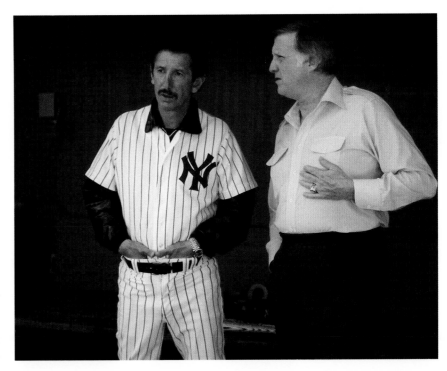

would return to manage the Yankees in 1980. Jackson was devastated.

But there was still the 1978 season. The calm Lemon established some normalcy and the Yankees began to roll. They cut Boston's once insurmountable 14-game lead to four games by September 7, and then, in the "Boston Massacre," whipped the Red Sox by scores of 15-3, 13-2, 7-0 and 7-4, and the AL East was deadlocked. By mid-September New York was sitting pretty with a three-and-a-half-game lead. But the Red Sox weren't quitting, either. They won all of their final eight games, and the two clubs finished with identical 99-63 records. The single playoff game for the division title would make for a memorable afternoon at Fenway Park.

Boston was leading, 2-0, when the Yankees rallied in the seventh for four runs, three of them coming on a Bucky Dent homer that had just enough carry to clear the high left-field wall. Then Jackson homered in the eighth, putting the Yankees up, 5-2. The Red Sox made it 5-4 in the bottom of the eighth, and in the ninth, Rick Burleson drew a one-out walk and Jerry Remy lined to right. Piniella lost the ball in the sun but refused to let Burleson know it and managed a one-hop recovery. With the decoy and quick recovery, he kept Burleson on second base. Jim Rice then skied out to Lou as Burleson, who would have easily scored to tie the game had he reached third on the Remy single, tagged and took third. With two outs and the Yankees' third straight division crown hanging by a thread, relief ace Goose Gossage retired the great Carl Yastrzemski on a pop-up.

There was little time to celebrate, how-

Above: *The bossmen, manager Billy Martin and the principal owner of the Yankees, George Steinbrenner. The latter fired the former no less than five times.*

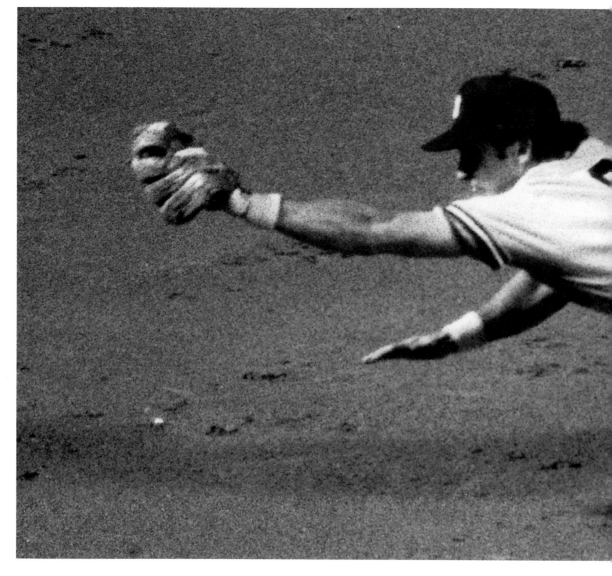

Right: *Graig Nettles became the talk of an admiring nation with his sparkling play at third base during the 1978 World Series. Here he stabs a shot in game two, and while he was unable to nail the Dodgers' hitter, Steve Garvey, he kept the hit from going for extra bases.*

ever, the Yankees speeding off to Kansas City and the Championship Series. They won the series in four games for their thirty-second American League flag. Jackson (two homers, six RBIs, .462 batting average) led the way, but a Munson homer won game three, and homers by Nettles and White gave Guidry a 2-1 victory in game four.

The 1978 World Series dealt the Yankees two quick defeats at the hands of the Dodgers. Guidry came back to win game three, 5-1, with Nettles making several sparkling plays at third base. In the sixth inning of game four, a relay intended to complete an inning-ending double play glanced off Jackson's hip and allowed Munson to score. Los Angeles vehemently argued that Jackson had deliberately deflected the ball, but the protests were in vain. The Yanks won the game, 4-3, on a tenth-inning Piniella single, and went on to hammer the Dodgers in the next two meetings, gaining their second straight World Championship and their twenty-second overall.

It was a World Series of great relief work by Gossage, unbelievable fielding by Nettles, and big contributions from two little guys, Bucky Dent (.417 batting average), the Series MVP, and Brian Doyle (.438 batting average), who filled in at second base for an injured Randolph. Jackson (two homers, eight RBIs, .391 batting average) provided much of the power, and his old Oakland teammate, Hunter, pitched seven strong innings to win the final game.

The win capped a miracle season for Hunter as well as for the Yankees. Catfish's career was in jeopardy until he had helped the Yanks get back in the race with a perfect 6-0 record in August; he was 12-6 in this, his next-to-last season. Figueroa won his last eight decisions and finished at 20-9. Gossage, a free agent pickup who threw nothing but smoke from behind an imposing scowl, led the league with 27 saves.

But with the possible exception of Jack Chesbro in his 1904 season, no Yankees hurler accomplished as much in one year as Ron Guidry did in 1978. The Cy Young Award winner posted a 25-3 record, including the playoff victory against Boston. He led the league in wins, establishing a major-league record for 20-game winners with an .893 winning percentage, and would go 2-0 in the post-season. He led the league in shutouts (nine) and ERA (1.74). He set a new Yankees record with 248 strikeouts – 18 of them in a single game against the Angels – breaking Chesbro's 1904 mark of 239.

Atley Donald had won his first 12 decisions for the Yankees in 1939 – another record broken by Guidry in 1978 – and it was Donald as a Yankees scout who had made Guidry the third selection in the 1971 draft. Guidry had followed a torturous and discouraging path through the Yankees farm system as a relief pitcher. He seriously considered quitting baseball, but his wife, Bonnie, urged him to give it one more try, and when Ron in 1977 got his chance in the Yanks' starting rotation, he didn't waste it. "Louisiana Lightning" was soon the most famous man Lafayette, Louisiana, had ever produced.

The Yankees were at the top of the baseball world, but tragedy lay ahead. Thurman Munson was killed in a plane crash on August 2, 1979. With the Yankees' logo on its side, his plane crashed several hundred feet from a runway at the Akron-Canton Airport. Two companions managed to get out of the burning aircraft, but Munson was trapped inside. Three weeks earlier, with Jackson and Nettles as passengers in his plane, Munson had complained that "nothing in this damn thing ever works completely right."

The news of the crash devastated Steinbrenner, Martin and the Yankee players. Munson was often gruff, but his friends knew him as a loyal friend and loving family man. Yankees fans who never had met Thurman remembered him as a bulldog competitor who seldom failed in the clutch. The entire team attended their captain's funeral in Canton, and Piniella and Bobby Murcer gave heartfelt eulogies. That night at Yankee Stadium a sleepless Murcer, having only two months earlier rejoined his friend Munson when the Yankees swung a deal for him with the Cubs, knocked in all New York's runs in a 5-4 defeat of Baltimore.

The 1979 Yankees didn't have that bad a record (89-71) but finished fourth, ending their three-year reign as league champs. Besides the late-season loss of their leader, Munson, the Yankees traded away players who had helped make the 1976-78 years

Above: *Rick Cerone, Thurman Munson's successor in 1980, caught well and hit .277, with 14 homers and 85 RBIs.*

Above right: *Oscar Gamble, an important factor in the Yanks' 1976 pennant year, was traded to the White Sox in 1977 for Bucky Dent.*

successful, including Lyle and Rivers. Maybe the fastest man ever to wear pinstripes, Rivers was wonderfully refreshing – when he was in the mood. He had a twitching, limping body language that was deceptive and articulate. And he was not so bad with the spoken language either. When Jackson claimed to have an I.Q. of 140, Mick the Quick asked: "Out of what? 1000?"

On June 19, 1979, the Yankees let Bob Lemon go and brought Martin back as manager. Billy was looking ahead to 1980, and then in late October, he was involved in an altercation with a marshmallow salesman in a Minnesota bar. Steinbrenner had had enough – the reign of Billy II was over. Dick Howser, head coach at Florida State University and a former player and recent coach with the Yanks, was named the new field boss.

Howser was sensational. Only four Yankees teams (1927, 1932, 1939 and 1961) ever won more games than the 103 games his 1980 Yankees won. He drew the best from Jackson, who enjoyed his finest Yankees season, hitting 41 homers and driving in 111 runs. Howser also exploited a deep Yankees bench, and while he made rookie mistakes, he brought a bright, winning attitude to the clubhouse. However,

his relations with Steinbrenner deteriorated badly – and publicly.

The 1980 season was a race with the Orioles, the previous year's pennant winner, who got off to a terrible start but by mid-summer were the hottest club in baseball. The Birds won six of eight meetings with the Yankees in August, and a nine-and-a-half-game Yankees lead would dwindle to a half game. Steinbrenner was not happy. But the Yankees hung tough and, beginning in late August, won 28 of their last 37 games, finishing three games in front of Baltimore.

The Yankees' power was distributed across nine pinstripers, each of whom hit at least 10 homers. They were, besides Jackson with 41, Nettles (16), outfielder Bobby Brown (14), catcher Rick Cerone (14), Gamble (14), Murcer (13), the first base-sharing Jim Spencer and Bob Watson (each 13), and designated hitter Eric Soderholm (11).

On the hill, the 1980 Yankees were led by veteran Tommy John, who had a 22-9 record. Not bad for a pitcher who only a few years earlier had undergone extensive arm reconstruction and was out of baseball for a year and a half. "The Bionic Arm" had joined the Yankees in 1979 as a free agent. Guidry (17-10), Rudy May (15-5) and Tom

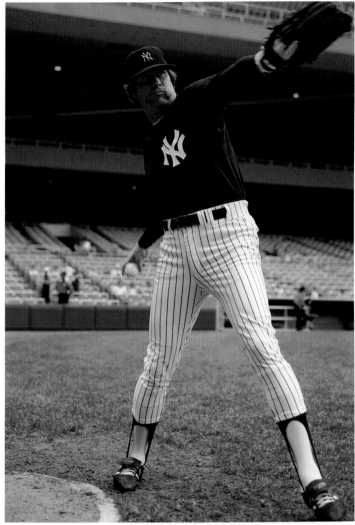

Underwood (13-9) rounded out the all-southpaw Big Four. The bullpen was what really made the 1980 Yankees special, the Yankees winning 77 of the 79 games in which they were leading going into the seventh inning. It was a deep bullpen, but it was great mostly because of the work of Ron Davis (9-3, 2.95 ERA, seven saves) and Gossage (6-2, 2.27 ERA, 33 saves). Davis set up Gossage, who over one seven-game stretch retired 28 hitters in a row. Goose was the most awesome relief pitcher in the game, his 100-mph fastball jumping and darting and riding – nearly impossible to hit. "The Goose is loose," Yankees fans would say, "and ready to produce."

Still, the formidable 1980 Yankees would meet disaster in the League Championship Series. For the fourth time in five years, they were pitted against Kansas City, and the Royals, sweeping aside previous disappointments, won in three straight, 7-2, 3-2 and 4-2. The Yankees lost their big chance in the eighth inning of game two. They were trailing, 3-2, with two out and Randolph on first. A Bob Watson double came up nicely to left fielder Willie Wilson, and Randolph, blazing toward third, was waved home by third base coach Mike Ferraro. George Brett, positioned behind the

cutoff man, accepted Wilson's overthrow and fired perfectly to the plate. Randolph was out. Steinbrenner was irate.

Soon thereafter Steinbrenner announced that the third-base coaching job was available if Don Zimmer wanted it. Howser said he wanted the courtesy of approving his coaches. It went back and forth until Howser was fired. Gene Michael, the former shortstop and the club's general manager, was named manager.

Michael's first year as manager was the tormented split-season of 1981. A players' strike interrupted the season on June 12 and play was suspended until August 10. So there were two seasons, the First and Second, but neither dominated the 1981 baseball story as much as the strike. The First Season-winning Yankees were part of a revised post-season playoff system. By then, however, "Stick" Michael had been replaced by Bob Lemon.

A fed-up Michael in August told the press he was tired of being threatened by the boss. If Steinbrenner wanted to fire him, he could go and do it. Steinbrenner waited for an apology, got none, and on September 6 canned Michael.

Steinbrenner also soured on Jackson, who slumped through the entire First Sea-

Above left: *Tommy John, in a 25-year big-league career which ended with the Yankees in 1989, was a 20-game winner three times – with the Dodgers in 1977 and the Yankees in 1979 and 1980 – enjoying his best years following reconstructive elbow surgery in 1974.*

Above: *Reliever Goose Gossage intimidated hitters with an explosive fastball, hulking frame, whiskered face and menacing scowl. Between 1978 and 1983 he set a Yankee record for most saves, later broken by Dave Righetti (188) and demolished by Mariano Rivera (413).*

son, and George's new Big Guy was Dave Winfield, the former Padre who as a free agent had signed a 10-year, multimillion-dollar contract with the Yankees. A three-sports star at the University of Minnesota, Winfield never played in the minors. With the Yankees he quickly showed himself as a smoking line-drive hitter, a daring, smart and swift baserunner, and an incredibly talented outfielder. He made a couple of catches above the left-field wall at Yankee Stadium the likes of which had never been seen. And he led the club with 68 RBIs.

Having bested Second Season-winning Milwaukee in the division playoffs – the Yankees in winning the First Season had gone 34-22 – the Yankees next faced Oakland for the American League pennant. Instead of Martin-hyphen-Lemon (the Yankees' managerial sequence in 1978), it was Martin-versus-Lemon, Martin having become the much-publicized "Billy Ball" manager of the A's. The Yankees won the League Championship Series in three games. Nettles (nine RBIs, .500 batting average) was the Series MVP and the adversary of Reggie Jackson in a mini-brawl during the pennant celebration. The two made up on their way to meet the Los Angeles Dodgers.

Right: *An exceptional right fielder, Dave Winfield intently follows the flight of a ball as an umpire prepares to make a call on the play at Yankee Stadium.*

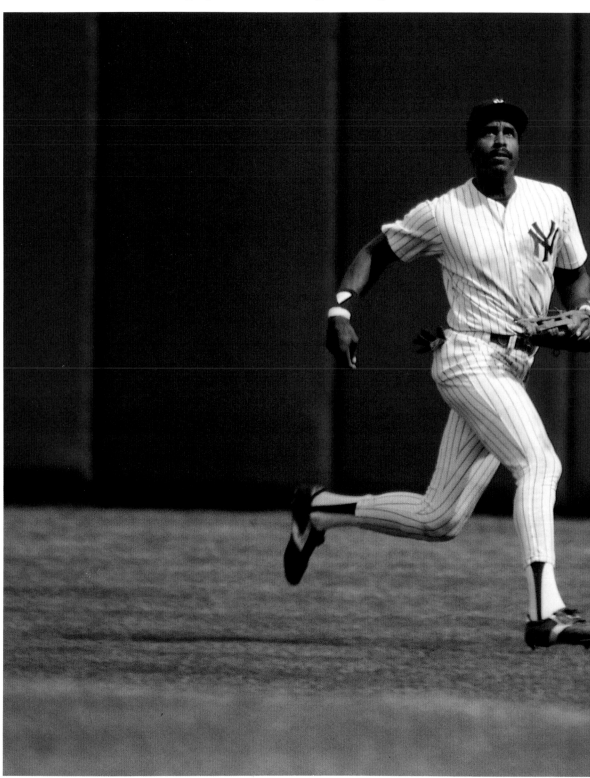

None other than Steinbrenner himself was to get into a tussle in the 1981 World Series. After the Yankees won the first two games and the Series moved to Los Angeles, the Dodgers began to win. Steinbrenner was on an elevator and, according to George, encountered a couple of Dodgers revelers who said nasty things about New York and the Yankees. With honor having to be upheld, the Yankees owner waded in and came out with a swollen lip and a broken hand.

But it would be for the Yankees losing the Series that Steinbrenner would apologize. "I've got nothing to apologize for," Jackson said. He cleared out his locker at Yankee Stadium for good. Had Steinbrenner, acting through Lemon, not iced him for game three, when a win would have put the Yankees up three games to none, Mr. October figured, the outcome might have been different. His sidelining in games one and two because of an injury was understandable, but he was ready and able to play in game three. He never got the chance. Steinbrenner wanted him to be "invisible" in this Series, Reggie would later assert. The Dodgers not only won game three but games four, five and six as well — and the 1981 World Championship.

8. Competitive, But Never Quite Complete

In the absence of a slugging Reggie Jackson, the Bronx Bombers in 1982 decided to become the Bronx Fighter Planes. The concept: to win with speed. Toward this end, Ken Griffey and Dave Collins were obtained by trade and free agency, but Griffey was disappointing, and Collins, as one of three Yankees assigned to first base, had

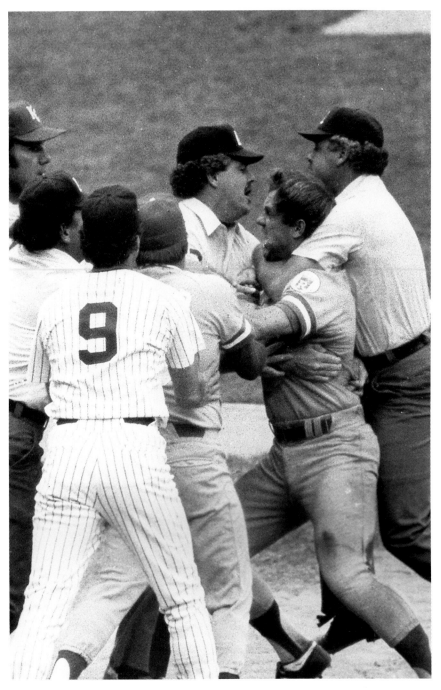

trouble getting on the field let alone the basepaths. The Yankees, who also had the greyhound-like Dave Winfield and the fleet Willie Randolph, did have speed, but they couldn't dominate through speed and make this latest of "new eras" work.

The Yankees finished fifth, but Winfield with 37 homers and 106 RBIs had a big year, and so did Goose Gossage (soon to break loose as a free agent), with 29 saves, and Ron Guidry, at 14-8. But the club (79-83) was never cohesive. Playing under three managers – Bob Lemon, Gene Michael and Clyde King – the Yankees kept spinning their wheels.

The Yankees returned to a familiar plan in 1983, the year of Billy III. They improved their record to 91-71 and finished third. Dave Righetti created a Fourth of July explosion at Yankee Stadium with a no-hitter against Boston, the Yankees' first since Don Larsen's perfect game in the 1956 World Series. When Rags struck out Wade Boggs for the final out, the crowd erupted in a wild, holiday celebration.

Righetti, a tall, good-looking son of Leo Righetti who played shortstop in the Yankees' farm system, had been acquired in the deal that sent Sparky Lyle to Texas, and he was the Rookie of the Year in 1981. His no-hitter year of 1983 – he was 14-8 on the year with a 3.44 ERA – was followed by a period of lively debate as to whether he should, or should not, be shifted to the bullpen. Probably the first to tire of the argument, Righetti would go to work and became an outstanding reliever.

The no-hitter was but one of several memorable events in 1983. There was the Yankees-Royals pine tar game at Yankee Stadium on July 24. Martin and the Yankees argued that George Brett, who hit a two-run, ninth-inning homer that gave the Royals a 5-4 lead, used a bat carrying pine tar that extended beyond the limit permitted by the rules. The umpires agreed, invalidated the homer and ruled Brett out. The game ended with the Yankees' 4-3 victors. The angry Royals took the case to the league office. Four days later President Lee MacPhail overruled his umpires and

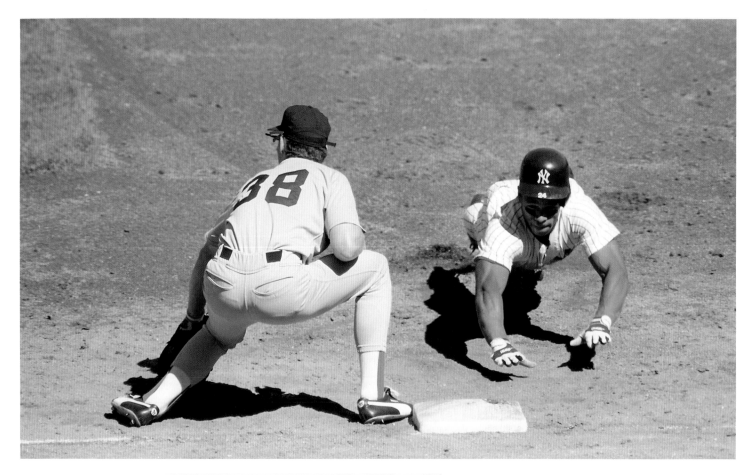

Above: *The all-time stolen-base leader of the Yankees, Rickey Henderson, gets back to first. Henderson swiped 93 in 1988.*

Right: *Yogi Berra, left, is introduced as the Yanks' manager for 1984 by George Steinbrenner, the Yankees' owner.*

declared the game suspended with the score 5-4 in favor of Kansas City, a score that stood up after the game was resumed August 18, the Yankees failing to push across a run with the three outs remaining to them. "We felt we had a game taken away from us," Martin said.

Then Winfield killed a seagull in Toronto and was arrested for cruelty to animals. In tossing a ball to a ball boy August 4, Winnie thought he'd bounce it near the bird to get it off the field. Instead, he cold-cocked it. The next thing the roundly-booed Winfield knew was that the police were waiting for him in the clubhouse. Down at the station, where the authorities had the bird, its feet upright, Winfield posted $500 bail on the charge that later was dropped.

The seagull incident brought some comic relief to the season's growing tensions, but what happened on August 18 was anything but funny. Shortstop Andre Robertson, the infield anchor with the fine arm, suffered a broken neck in an auto accident. The rangy, graceful Robertson would never play again.

The curtain came down on Billy III with the season's close. Yogi Berra would be the manager in 1984, but before Berra could look up the Tigers preempted a pennant race by leaping to a 35-5 start. But Yankees fans were treated to a battle between two of their own, Dave Winfield and Don Mattingly, who competed for the league batting championship into the last game of the season, with Winfield leading, .3410 to .3394. Mattingly went four for five that day and Winfield one for four; Mattingly emerged the batting champion at .343, Winfield finishing at .340.

In only his first full campaign, Mattingly was suddenly the premier first baseman in baseball. Called "the best Yankee first baseman I have seen in 40 years" by Phil Rizzuto, he was among the league leaders in a half dozen offensive categories. He not only hit for average but he hit for distance (23 homers) and drove in runs (110 RBIs).

Mattingly had given a clue as to what might be expected of him in his 91 games with New York the previous season, looking good around the bag, hitting .283 and showing a sweet stroke. A hard worker, he evoked memories of the industrious Lou Gehrig. He would hit .352 in 1986, only to place second to Boston's Wade Boggs, who batted a stunning .357. In that season's final set, at Fenway Park, Mattingly, the Yankees' new Big Guy, went 8 for 19; in his pursuit of Boggs he collected his fifty-third double and 238th hit to beat, respectively, club records of Lou Gehrig and Earle Combs.

Winfield had a fine all-around 1984. He had a 20-game hitting streak and 100 RBIs, and he won his third straight Gold Glove, all this while in a season-long battle with Steinbrenner over a feature of his contract, the David M. Winfield Foundation, and the owner's payments to the foundation which assists youths and the community. There were times when he felt like accepting the trade he said the Yankees kept pressuring him to take.

The Yankees in 1985 got off to a 6-10 start, bringing the axe down on Berra; the grinding up of a great old Yankee further alienated Steinbrenner from the fans. The players liked the easy-going Berra and weren't happy to see him go. If they liked him so much, Steinbrenner said, ushering in Billy IV, they should have won for him.

One player who was doubtless happy to see Martin was the newest Yankee, speed merchant Rickey Henderson, who had flourished under Billy at Oakland in 1982, setting a single-season record for stolen bases with 130. Perhaps the greatest lead-off man in baseball history, Henderson's job with the Yankees was to create havoc on

Above: *Veteran Phil Niekro won 16 games for New York in 1984 and again in 1985.*

Left: *The Yanks' Don Mattingly was down by seven points in the race for the batting title going into the 1986 season's final series in Boston. Wade Boggs of the Red Sox was the winner with .357; Mattingly, shown with the winner in Fenway Park, came in a close second with a .352 average.*

the bases, score runs and cover center field.

The 1985 Yankees had the spirited horses – principally, Henderson, Mattingly, Winfield – to win the title, and with Martin driving them, were in the race until the next-to-the-last day of the season. But a fine 97-64 record qualified for only second place. Something happened to the Yankees in September; it seemed that owner and management pressure momentarily squelched their ability to win.

Their inability to win stretched over eight games, a downturn that coincided with Steinbrenner's sharp, goading criticism. Had it not been for the criticism, the Yankees just might have been in a better position for the season's final three games with the Blue Jays, who led New York by exactly three games. The Yankees still had a shot at sweeping and forcing a one-game playoff, and they did win the first game. But Toronto's Doyle Alexander had them in his

pocket in the second game, and it was over, for everyone but the Yanks' Phil Niekro, who in the final game racked up his 300th big-league victory.

The Yankees of 1985 failed to win the pennant, but Don Mattingly won an MVP, the unbridled approval of Yankees fans and the admiration of baseball fans. He was suddenly baseball's best player. He led the majors with 145 RBIs and 48 doubles. He led the American League with 370 total bases, 86 extra-base hits and 21 game-winning RBIs. He had 211 hits, 107 runs, 35 homers, a .567 slugging percentage, a .324 batting average and a Gold Glove.

Among the top 15 MVP vote-getters along with Mattingly (367 points) were Yankees Rickey Henderson (174), Dave Winfield (35) and Ron Guidry (15). Henderson (24 homers, 72 RBIs, .314 batting average) took off like a rocket. Not only did he steal 80 bases but his 146 runs scored was also the highest single-season major-league total since Ted Williams' 150 in 1949. Winfield (26 homers, 114 RBIs, 105 runs) exceeded 100 RBIs and 100 runs for the second straight season. Guidry, after a 10-11 season in 1984, reestablished himself as a star with a sparkling 22-6 season, the third 20-win season for Louisiana Lightning. Holy Cow!

Phil Rizzuto, the former Yankees short-stop and a Yankee radio-TV announcer for more than three decades, was known as the Holy Cow man in New York. It is an expression borrowed from Earl Gillespie, who once did the Braves' games, and the engaging Phil used it like a short order cook uses salt. Rizzuto is the Yankees as Yankee Stadium is the Yankees, as the late Pete Sheehy, beloved clubhouse man for over 50 years, was the Yankees, as the dignified voice of Bob Sheppard, the Yankee Stadium PA announcer, is the Yankees. Yankees haters dislike Rizzuto; he wore his Yankees allegiance, yet he could be fairer than some announcers who wear a pretense of objectivity. Rizzuto was a character; his "Holy Cow" didn't tell the listener whether the ball left the park or was in somebody's glove. No problem – the facts emerged in time. To many a listener, Rizzuto was at least as important as baseball.

On Phil Rizzuto Day at Yankee Stadium in 1985, the Scooter's uniform number, 10, was retired. Earlier in the year the Yankees retired numbers 9 and 32, the numbers of Roger Maris, who would die of cancer in December, and Elston Howard, who died in 1980. Time was marching on. Old favorites were passing on.

Old favorite Billy Martin wouldn't be back with the Yankees in 1986 – a repercussion of his ugly bar brawl with pitcher Ed Whitson in the heat of the September pen-

Below: Phil Rizzuto's number 10 is retired on his "day" at Yankee Stadium in 1985.

Opposite: *The Yanks' new manager for 1986, Lou Piniella, has a beef with the umps.*

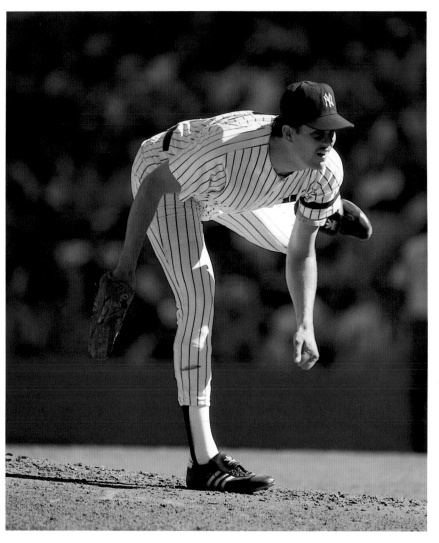

Above: *The winner of 18 games in 1986, Dennis Rasmussen was 9-7 in mid-1987 when he was optioned to Columbus. Later he was dealt to San Diego.*

who posted 46 saves. Righetti exceeded by one the big-league record shared by Dan Quisenberry and Bruce Sutter.

The Yankees won 89 games and finished fourth in the revolving-door year of 1987. They used 48 players, 15 of them as starting pitchers. However, Piniella had his team in first place at the All-Star break, the Yanks sporting an excellent 55-34 record. But the Yankees fell apart in August (11-17). Injuries mounted and unwise personnel decisions were made. A July trade for Steve Trout, thought to be pennant insurance, was probably the biggest blunder; a hopelessly wild Trout would go 0-4 in New York. And on top of this, Steinbrenner was arguing that he gave Piniella all he wanted, adding that the one thing he didn't give Lou, and maybe should have, was minor-league managerial experience. Saddled with a 4.36 ERA pitching staff, Piniella never had a chance.

Steinbrenner by this time had made himself one of the most famous Yankees ever. Having long since passed Chesbro on the club's All-Time Well-Known List, he was pressing the Bambino himself. Intense Yankees fans may be riveted to batting averages and what the Columbus Clippers may have in their bag for the Big Club, but the Yankees' story to the casual public was Steinbrenner. One group's steward is another's celebrity.

The winning ways that George Steinbrenner brought to Yankee Stadium felt good after the long years of drought. He did what it took to build a winner; his style and excesses could be excused. But the Yankees hadn't won anything for nearly a decade. Accordingly, the Steinbrenner style, which commonly is seen as dictatorial, is much less tolerable.

Had Steinbrenner lost some of his zeal for conquest – that is, for recruiting conquerors? Often bemoaning the big money he paid his players, he said things like, "I'm sure as hell not making millions of dollars a year *playing a game*." Had his ardor for getting game players cooled? While he lost no time in netting Catfish Hunter, he passed up Jack Morris, who for two years was available as a free agent and who finally re-signed with Detroit. Usually around the 20-win mark, the Tiger pitcher drew no interest. Nor did Steinbrenner show any interest in Mike Boddicker of the Orioles, who in 1988 was picked up by Boston, or even in retaining Claudell Washington following the 1988 season, which he could have done for a mere $200,000. Over the 1988-89 off-season, Nolan Ryan and Bruce Hurst were on the open market, but neither pitcher was signed by New York. In mid-1989 the Twins traded pitcher Frank

nant drive. Sweet Lou Piniella would hold the reins in 1986. Piniella, a Floridian of Spanish descent who played a hustling outfield and hit .295 in 11 Yankees seasons (1974-84), should have been the Manager of the Year in 1986, according to Billy Martin. Billy said Piniella deserved the honor because of "the way he kept the team in the race, with all the pitching problems he faced. . . ." Lou had been one of the Yankees' most popular players. He had played with emotion and he played to win. He was a scientific hitter, great in the clutch. He never made his outfield chores look easy, but he got them done. Most of his players liked him as a manager, although possibly because of his pitching woes, he was less sweet than "Sweet Lou," the player.

The pitching staff compiled an ERA of 4.11 in 1986, the first season Yankees pitchers had allowed better than four runs a game in 36 years. Guidry and Joe Niekro had off years and Whitson would be dealt to San Diego in mid-season. The Yankees won 90 games, but lacking consistent pitching, they never made a serious run at the pennant, and finished second. Dennis Rasmussen (18-6) was the big winner, but the real star of the mound corps was Dave Righetti,

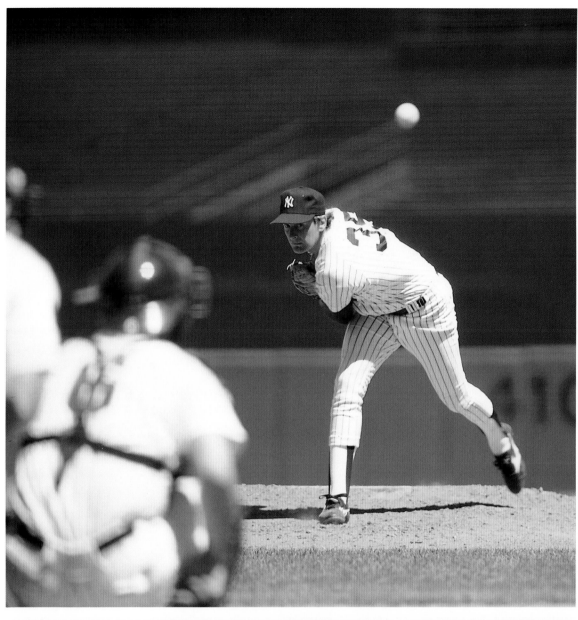

Left: *Steve Trout was obtained in July 1987 to counter New York's mound woes, but he couldn't keep control of his offerings.*

Below: *Meanwhile, the self-expression that is inevitable in a city like New York made itself apparent.*

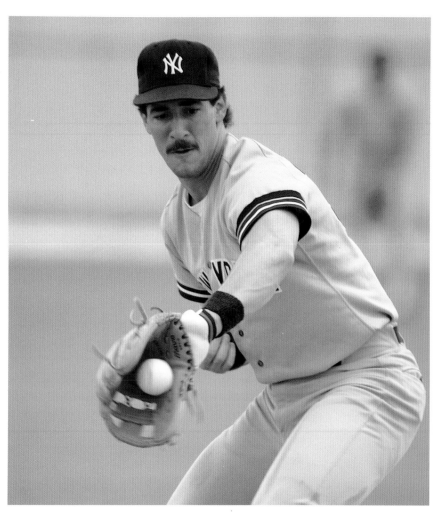

Viola to New York – to the Mets, not the Yankees.

Baseball, without pitching, is throwing the ball and watching others have fun. The 1987 year was not a particularly happy one for the Yankees' camp. Mattingly (30 homers, 115 RBIs, .327 batting average) tried to cheer it up, hitting home runs in eight consecutive games and blasting a big-league record six grand slams. Righetti made merry with 31 saves, and Pagliarulo joined in with 32 homers. But Piniella was a goner. Martin would be the field boss in 1988. The gloom of the Yankees' Dark Ages had given way to a Renaissance, and the Renaissance was now giving way to the giggles. Billy V? Said Billy: "The last laugh is going to be mine."

Billy was rejoined with the old cast and another new Big Guy, Jack Clark. A free agent signed to a two-year contract, Clark was a feared slugger, and some believed that adding the former Cardinal to a lineup that already boasted Henderson, Mattingly, Winfield and Pagliarulo might make it possible for the Yankees to blast their way to the top, and maybe, just maybe, get to play the prospering Mets in a Subway Series.

The 1988 Mets would win their division race but lose in the playoffs; the 1988

Above: *Third baseman Mike Pagliarulo was traded in 1989.*

Right: *Jack Clark, too, was traded away in 1989. Like Bobby Bonds before him, Clark spent a year with the Yankees but never made much of a difference. Both Pagliarulo and Clark were traded to San Diego.*

Left: *Steve Sax had a superb 1989 season at second base, taking some of the sting out of the departure of Willie Randolph.*

Yankees would fuss and fight to a fifth-place finish. Martin's last laugh, for a while, was on schedule, Billy holding New York in first place from May 3 through June 20. He was only two games out on June 23 when Piniella replaced him. Billy had been feuding with the umpires, but his biggest indiscretion had to do with a fight in a Texas topless bar and the conflicting accounts of what had happened.

Piniella would guide the Yankees back into first place briefly in late July, and even though they swooned again in August (9-20), they stayed alive until Boston dealt them three smashing defeats in mid-September. These 85-76 Yankees finished three and a half games behind first-place Boston. Clark played well, hitting 27 homers and driving in 93 runs, but the awesome attack his presence was to help foster never materialized.

While seemingly unable to land quality pitchers, the Yankees had been busy in pursuit of so-so hurlers. In December of 1988 they signed free agents Andy Hawkins and Dave LaPoint. Hawkins would be up and down in 1989, and LaPoint, when not hurt, was often ineffective. Two Steinbrenner invitees to spring camp separated from the club, Ron Guidry retiring with a lifetime record of 170-91, and 45-year-old Tommy John, who made the club and even pitched the season opener, accepting his release but not the end of his career.

Pitching would remain New York's biggest headache in 1989. And yet, such former Yankees pitchers as Rick Reuschel, Dennis Rasmussen, Doyle Alexander, Ed Whitson, Shane Rawley and Jay Howell were going strong with other teams. Worse, good pitchers who were developed in the Yankees' farm system – Jose Rijo, Jim Deshaies and Gene Nelson – were busy laboring elsewhere.

The Yankees, trying to tape together a mound staff, seemed to lack a consistent personnel policy. Indeed, their only front office constant was Steinbrenner. The Yankees of the 1980s had eight general managers, 12 managers and 20 pitching coaches. Apparently convinced that the club wasn't getting its money's worth from its hurlers, Steinbrenner used pitching coaches like kleenexes.

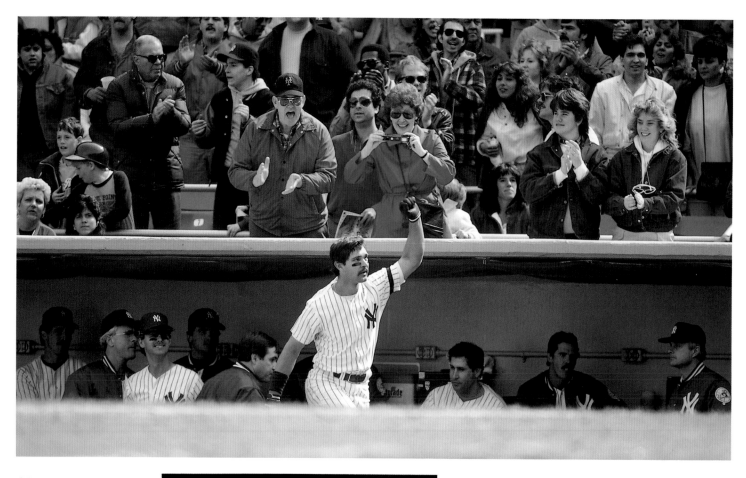

Above: *Don Mattingly acknowledges the fans' appreciation.*

Right: *Catcher Don Slaught waits with manager Dallas Green for the next Yankee pitcher to reach the mound, a scene often repeated in 1989.*

Gone along with Guidry in 1989 was Willie Randolph – the two were the last remaining players from the great 1977-78 World Championship teams. Randolph played out his option in 1988 after 13 sea-

sons in pinstripes. Willie had been the rock-solid, silent star of the Yankees, a five-time All-Star second baseman who did everything well except hit for power. And amid the controversy swirling about the Yankees throughout his career, Willie, while not immunized, maintained a detached dignity. He signed with the Dodgers after the Yankees signed free-agent second baseman Steve Sax, formerly of the Dodgers, in November 1988. Both second basemen made their respective league's All-Star teams in 1989.

The Yankees' 1989 manager, Dallas Green, not only inherited a festering pitching situation but had unexpected lineup problems as well. Jack Clark was gone, having been traded for a couple of pitchers. Dave Winfield underwent surgery for a herniated disk and was lost for the year. Rickey Henderson was asking for a new contract and was setting a timetable. Henderson was great in pinstripes – but a feeling persisted that he could have done more, like play hurt and hustle after balls that got by him. He wasn't setting the world on fire, so the Yankees in mid-season traded Henderson to Oakland, where he began setting the world on fire. They would also trade away hard-working, hard-hitting, good-glove Mike Pagliarulo, leaving a big hole at third base. To fill Winfield's defensive and right-handed power roles, the Yankees acquired three players – Mel Hall, Jesse Barfield and Steve Balboni – each of whom, while playing well, showed a deficiency or two in his game.

The AL East was uncharacteristically weak in 1989. The Yankees could have pulled away from this mediocrity with one of their teams from earlier in the 1980s, but with their 1989 club the big goal was just to get to .500 baseball. For a time, the Yankees remained in the race all the same, up until another pathetic August exposed them as pretenders, not contenders, the pitching proving even worse than in the recent past. Among the regulars, only Mattingly (another 100-plus RBI season), Sax, young Roberto Kelly and shortstop Alvaro Espinoza had good years.

Dallas Green was tough, caustic and quick to criticize his players. He had lost confidence in Pagliarulo, who was being platooned and who pressed when he did get to play. He emphasized game-situation baseball. He paced the clubhouse for 10 minutes after one particularly painful Yankees defeat, distressed that the Yankees "need 10 hits, 16 passed balls and 10 errors before we can score a run." Added Green, "It's pretty obvious the guys don't understand what game-situation baseball is. We had a chance to win that game 50 times." The May 16 game went to California, 4-3, in 11 innings.

Green, who in 1980 managed the Phillies to a World Championship, gave the feeling all along that he expected to be fired; he also gave the feeling that he could live with that expectation. He was critical of more than his players, finding fault in mid-season with Steinbrenner. And the principal owner also found fault with manager Green, unsurprisingly.

Green and Steinbrenner bickered through the press for a few weeks, and as the Yankees faded in August, Green faded from pinstripes. A short time later Syd Thrift, vice president in charge of personnel, and a baseball man whose presence

Left: *Roberto Kelly, promising young center fielder for the Yankees, takes a good cut. Kelly was one of the few bright spots on the 1989 Yankees.*

Right: *Alvaro Espinoz takes a cut. The Yankee shortstop turned in a good 1989 season both in the field and at the plate.*

offered hope for a long-range talent strategy, resigned. Thrift became a casualty after only months in his Yankees job, apparently for his failure to give vocal support to Steinbrenner's canning of Green.

Into this mess – and the Yankees indeed were now as feeble and disorganized as the last-place club of 1966 – ventured a new manager, Bucky Dent. The club kept playing aimlessly, but then a sudden, surprising, nine-game Yankees winning streak solidified Dent's position and it was announced that Bucky would remain as manager. Being the manager of the

Yankees, however, is like being married to Henry VIII, although in the end there never was a Billy VI.

Eight years without a post-season team and 11 without a championship, Steinbrenner was again summoning Yankee history for inspiration. By anointing Dent, whose poke over the Green Monster devastated Boston in the 1978 playoff game, the majority owner sought the same managerial magic he'd prayed for in earlier Yankee heroes Berra, Martin and Piniella. But symbols alone wouldn't restore ancient Yankee glory. Better players were needed as well.

Above left: *Bucky Dent, shortly after assuming the managerial reins from Dallas Green near the end of the '89 campaign.*

Above: *Steve Balboni at the plate. The Yanks acquired Balboni in 1989 to help make up for the loss of injured Dave Winfield's bat.*

Left: *New Yankees Eric Plunk, Luis Polonia and Greg Cadaret pose at Yankee Stadium the day after being acquired from Oakland in exchange for Rickey Henderson.*

9. Titletown Once More

Above: *Rightfielder Paul O'Neill arrived from Cincinnati to spearhead four Yankee championships in five years.*

The 1990 Yankees began a new decade with perhaps their worst team ever. Fielding a young club averaging 28.2 years in age, they finished dead last in the American League's East Division with baseball's worst (67-95) record, a full 21 games behind the Red Sox. It was their first last-place finish since 1966. No one in the league hit worse than the Yankees' team average, .241. Roberto Kelly led the team with a .285 average — and had 148 strikeouts. Jesse Barfield hit 25 homers but batted only .246 and whiffed 150 times, the worst in Yankee history until Alfonso Soriano whiffed 157 times in 2002. Even Don Mattingly slumped — literally, because his back was killing him — with a .256 average, five homers and 42 runs batted in. Hall of Fame outfielder Dave Winfield batted .213 over 38 games and was traded to the Angels on May 11. "The lanky and controversial outfielder at first balked at the trade and then realized the Yankees

were doing him a favor," wrote baseball historian Harvey Frommer.

Tim Leary's nine wins led the starters, and his 19 losses led the league. Other players, including Bob Geren and Alan Mills, are best remembered by Yankee trivia experts. It was the kind of season in which Andy Hawkins would become the first Yankee pitcher to lose a no-hitter, going down 4-0 to the White Sox on three errors and two walks in the eighth. The snake-bit Hawkins faced the White Sox 11 days later, when the Yankees were no-hit over six innings in a rain-shortened game. The situation cried out for action from owner George Steinbrenner, but what he did was telling. With the team 18-31 on June 6, he axed manager Bucky Dent and replaced him with Stump Merrill from Triple-A Columbus. "Here we have a fellow who doesn't come with a whole lot of glamour," Steinbrenner said. "For the first five years I knew him, I kept calling him 'Lump.' He was madder than hell."

Steinbrenner could be excused for the misnomer, because his mind was no doubt elsewhere. On June 30, commissioner Fay Vincent banned him from day-to-day operations because he dealt with a known gambler, Howard Spira. Steinbrenner hired Spira to dig up dirt on Winfield, with whom The Boss had been feuding. Spira failed, but word of the arrangement got out. As the league's first owner removed for disciplinary reasons, Steinbrenner resigned as managing general partner and watched the remainder of the miserable season as the Yankees' glummest fan. And he got glummer. On July 5, the Yankees were fined $25,000 and ordered to pay the Angels $200,000 because Steinbrenner interfered in the Winfield trade.

Were there any bright spots? Yes. Dave Righetti had 36 saves, and the team's lone All-Star, second baseman Steve Sax, stole 43 bases. On August 2, rookie Kevin Maas hit the tenth homer in his first 77 at-bats, the soonest any player reached double figures in baseball history. "He fizzled, but at least he flamed out for a while," Frommer wrote, "which was more than could be said for a lot of other 1990 Yanks."

The team had not yet begun to win and hadn't begun to spend either, because their $19 million payroll wasn't the game's highest. In 1991 they improved to 71-91 and fifth place, with their lone All-Star Scott Sanderson going 16-10, but no other Yankee was among the league leaders. Overall, it was another unhappy year, especially when Merrill incurred the wrath of the popular Mattingly for insisting he have his hair trimmed. Merrill was fired on October 7, and two months later Robert Nederlander, who had replaced Steinbrenner as the team's managing general partner, resigned.

Under new manager Buck Showalter, the 1992 Yankees began building from within their farm system rather than using minor leaguers as trade bait. They continued inching up—42-45 at the All-Star break before finishing 76-86 in a tie for fourth place—but Yankee fever hadn't caught on. The team drew 1,748,737 fans at Yankee Stadium, just eleventh best in the 14-team league. Achievements of players like outfielder designated hitter Danny Tartabull (25 homers, 85 RBI, 103 walks) and pitcher Melido Perez (218 strikeouts) were too subtle to make them fan favorites. Nor did news that Steinbrenner would be reinstated the following season inspire anyone.

Perhaps inspired by Reggie Jackson's election to the Hall of Fame, the 1993 Yankees finally played like the Bombers of old. They finished in second with an 88-74 record, thanks in part to newcomers like Jimmy Key (18-6), Wade Boggs (.302) and Paul O'Neill (.311, 20 HR). A career .259 hitter in Cincinnati, O'Neill especially blossomed in his new city, where his sister Molly was a food critic for *The New York Times* and the fans loved his hard-nosed approach. In the team's best single-game showing, Jim Abbott, the noted one-handed pitcher late of California, no-hit Cleveland, 4-0.

The 1994 Yankees were poised for titledom with a first-place 70-43 record when a players' strike followed by an owners' lockout ended the season and cancelled the postseason. O'Neill led the league with a .359 average, Key had the most wins (17) and Showalter was Manager of the Year at age 38, small consolation for New York's title-starved fans. No season could pass, it seemed, without some embarrassment emanating from the front office. This time Richard Kraft,

vice president for community relations, resigned after a magazine article alleged that he used the terms "monkeys" and "colored boys" to describe black youths living near Yankee Stadium.

The 1995 season started late, following another player strike and spring-training games played by scabs. And the Yankees started sluggishly with a 30-36 record. Then they accelerated into mid-season form and finished like Secretariat by winning 26 of their last 33 games. With O'Neill, Boggs and Bernie Williams all hitting over .300 and new closer John Wetteland saving 31 games, they placed second to Boston with a 79-65 record in the shortened season and reached the playoffs as the league's first

Above: *Joe Torre led the Yankees to four World Series championships in his first five years (1996-2000), but after failing to top even the American League between 2004-2007, he left the team.*

wild-card team. The July 29 acquisition of pitcher David Cone, who went 9-2 down the stretch, was critical.

A five-game divisional series followed against Seattle that is still among baseball's most memorable. Playing the first two games at home, the Yankees won both, with Jim Leyritz's two run, walk-off homer in the fifteenth inning of game two — we'll be hearing more from him —giving them a 7-5 victory. In Seattle, the Mariners won twice, setting up a classic finale. The Yankees led 4-2 before Seattle tied the game in the eighth. Randy Velarde's run-scoring single gave New York a 5-4 lead in the eleventh. In the bottom half of the inning, Joey Cora and Ken Griffey, Jr., singled, and Edgar Martinez scored both of them with a series-ending double off Jack McDowell, a starter pressed into service to replace Rivera. The 6-5 loss was a heartbreaking conclusion for the 1995 Yankees.

Only a little less upsetting was the October 26 resignation of Showalter. He and Steinbrenner had been at odds over Showalter's handling of his bullpen; Steinbrenner even went so far as to praise Seattle manager Lou Piniella during the playoffs. When Showalter, whose contract was expiring, refused

the club's first salary offer, the pressure on him increased. The final straw was Showalter's refusal to follow Steinbrenner's orders and fire batting coach Rick Downs.

Few expected the 1996 Yankees to win their first World Series in 18 years. For one thing, little-appreciated figures supplanted popular Yankees, at the helm and on the field: Manager Joe Torre, first baseman Tino Martinez, and catcher Joe Girardi replacing Showalter, Mattingly and Mike Stanley, respectively. Torre was recommended to Steinbrenner by team official Arthur Richman. For another, a rookie named Derek Jeter was entrusted with the awesome responsibility of playing shortstop at Yankee Stadium.

And yet, the improbable happened. Despite one divisional title, no postseason wins and a .471 winning percentage in 14 previous managing seasons, Torre ("Clueless Joe," according to New York back pages) suggested that a championship might be possible and discovered to his delight that the players agreed. The talented staff Torre brought in included bench coach Don Zimmer and pitching coach Mel Stottlemyre; Torre retained respected third base coach Wil-

Below: *First baseman Tino Martinez was a power-hitting fixture in a latter-day version of the old Murderers Row.*

Left: *Since joining the Yankees in 1995, Mariano Rivera has taken over virtually every Yankee relief record and won numerous American League and post-season awards.*

lie Randolph. But it was Torre's smooth, cool manner that made an immediate difference. His understated, dignified approach proved to be the perfect counterpoint to the volatile character at the helm of the franchise. Torre put himself between the owner's rages and the players he raged at. All that Phineas T. Bluster seemed to dissipate when passed through the Yoda-like manager. The players could only appreciate him.

Because Torre was straight with his players and didn't show them up by communicating through the media, he immediately sublimated egos and earned respect. At Torre's urging, Steinbrenner eventually left most baseball decisions to his baseball men. By late April Torre had inserted a key piece into the puzzle by establishing Mariano Rivera as set-up man for closer John Wetteland. Given a second chance by Steinbrenner after problems with substance abuse, Dwight Gooden threw a 2-0 no-hitter at the Mariners on May 14. In June Torre was burdened by news of one brother dying of a heart attack and another needing a heart transplant. Nonetheless, with the uncompromising O'Neill providing

leadership to go with his .411 on-base percentage and veteran second baseman Mariano Duncan adding the mantra "We play today, we win today, das it," to his .340 average and .975 fielding average, the Yankees built up a 12-game lead by July 29. When it shrank to two on September 16, general manager Bob Watson suggested that he and Torre should be jettisoned if the lead didn't hold up.

Not to worry. Returning from a four-month absence after May 10 surgery for an aneurysm in his left armpit, Cone threw seven no-hit innings in his first outing back and the Yankees finished first with a 92-70 record, four games ahead of the Orioles. Though hardly harboring another Murderers Row, O'Neill, centerfielder Bernie Williams (.305, 29 HR, 102 RBI) and first baseman Tino Martinez (.292, 25, 117) struck fear in opposing pitchers. Only starting to draw comparisons to Whitey Ford, lefthander Andy Pettitte led the league with a 21-8 record. Wetteland was no Dennis Eckersley, but he had an AL-best 43 saves.

Though the extraordinary Jeter, who batted .314, looked like Phil Rizzuto and more, it was not big names that got

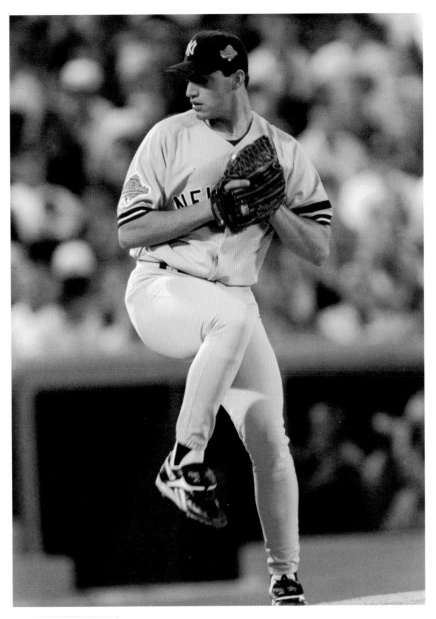

Above: *In his years with the Yankees, Andy Pettitte (1995-2003, 2007) has compiled a most respectable 164-87 record and should continue to aid the team in 2008.*

the Yanks to the postseason. Using the National League-style baseball he had learned as a player and skipper, Manager of the Year Torre's team beat the Orioles' juggernaut offense with what baseball people call "small ball." The Orioles had a clear-cut advantage in homers (257-162) and runs (949-871), but the Yankees bested them in batting average (.288-.274), on-base percentage (.360-.350), stolen bases (96-76) and every significant pitching category. It was baseball a baseball purist could appreciate. Still, it took contributions from unexpected sources before the Yankees could hoist another flag. After beating Texas three games to one in the divisional series — Cecil Fielder, another former star happy to be a role player, got the series-winning RBI—New York faced Baltimore for the American League championship.

And the Yankees might well have lost the opener if not for a happy case of kismet wrapped in karma. With the Yankees trailing the Orioles 4-3 in the eighth inning, Jeter hit a long fly to right field. As Tony Tarasco camped by the wall, schoolboy Jeffrey Maier stuck out his glove and deflected the ball into the stands. Umpire Richie Garcia blew the call, ruling home run instead of out by fan interference, and the game was tied. After the Orioles protested futilely, MVP Williams won it 5-4 with a walk-off homer in the eleventh. "I didn't mean to do anything bad," said Maier, who subsequently appeared on TV talk shows, got free tickets to game two from the New York *Daily News* and went on to become a star outfielder at Wesleyan College. "I'm just a 12-year-old kid trying to catch a ball."

Without Maier's timely assist, the Yanks might have gone down two games to none because the Orioles took the second game 5-2. As it was, New York took three straight to win the ALCS 4-1. Torre went to his first World Series after 36 years and a record 4,272 games as a player and manager, and the Yanks entered their first Fall Classic since 1981, this time against the powerful Atlanta Braves.

When the Yankees were pounded 12-1 in the opener at the Stadium and 19-year-old rookie Andruw Jones became the youngest player to homer in a World Series (he had two downtowners), Steinbrenner visited Torre before game two and told him the Yankees better win. "I told him, 'Don't worry about it. We might even lose tonight,'" Torre told *The New York Times*'s Jack Curry. "'But we're going to Atlanta. That's my town. We'll win three there and come back here and win it for you on Saturday.'"

Sure enough, the Yankees lost game two, 4-0, on a combined shutout by Greg Maddux and Mark Wohlers. And sure enough, they rebounded in Atlanta. First, the redoubtable Cone beat the Braves 5-2. Then, through five innings of game four, Atlanta built up a 6-0 lead; a win would almost surely doom the Yankees. New York chipped away for three runs in the sixth. But it was still 6-3 in the eighth when the little-used Leyritz came to bat with two men on. Leyritz swung. "In the air to left field," TV announcer Joe Buck called. "Back, at the track, at the wall, we are tied!" Thanks to another improbable October hero, the Yanks were back. "They're dancing in the streets in New York right now," Buck's broadcast partner Tim McCarver added. The Yankees won 8-6 in 10 innings on a bases-loaded walk to Boggs and an error. Leyritz's hit plainly shifted the Series' momentum.

But barely. Pettitte, the humiliated loser in game one, outdueled National

League Cy Young Award-winner John Smoltz, 1-0, in game five. Give assists to Pettitte for a pickoff and two fine fielding plays, as well as an eighth-inning, fence-crashing grab by another Steinbrenner rehab project, Darryl Strawberry, and a ninth-inning, game-ending stab by O'Neill, limping on a torn hamstring, who ran down a ball in the gap to prevent two runners from scoring. Back at Yankee Stadium after going 8-0 on the road in the postseason, game two loser Jimmy Key beat Maddux and the Braves 3-2 to win the Series four games to two, with an O'Neill double, a Joe Girardi triple, a single and steal by Jeter and a single by Williams giving the winners a three-run third. MVP Wetteland, who saved every precarious victory, gave up three hits and one run before escaping a tense ninth. It was the Yankees' 23rd world championship and their first since 1978. No one had ever before won the Series after losing the first two games at home.

When Mark Lemke fouled out to third baseman Charlie Hayes for the final out, the Yankees and their fans staged an especially boisterous celebration. It isn't every day that the Yankees win it all as underdogs. Though they didn't know it, they had just started another dynasty.

Below: *In his 16 years with the Yankees (1991-2006) as an outfielder and designated hitter, Bernie Williams set several records, won numerous awards and was a favorite of the fans.*

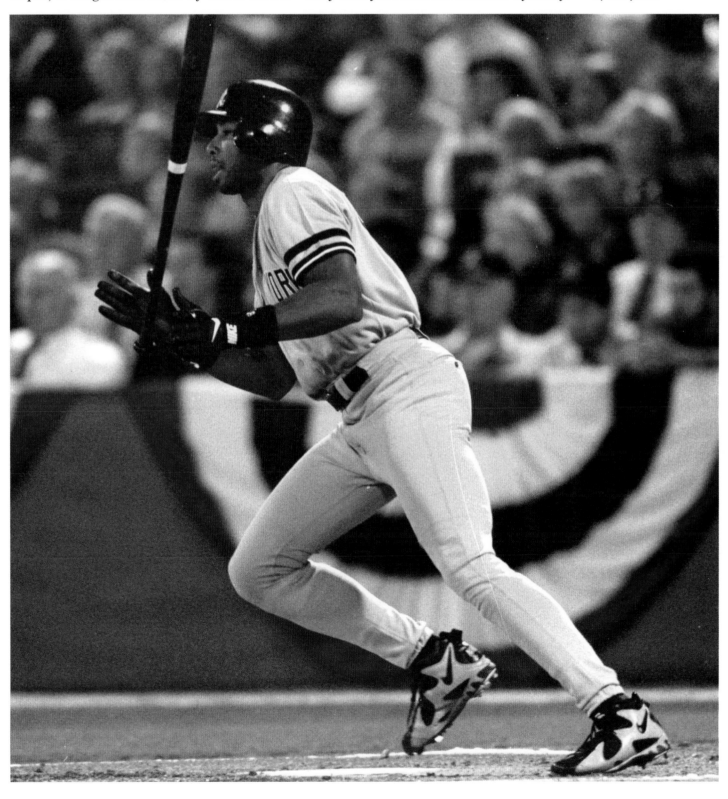

10. The Last Baseball Dynasty?

By most indices, the 1997 Yankees looked like an improved team. They signed experienced lefthander David Wells and proven reliever Mike Stanton, let John Wetteland go to free agency and promoted Mariano Rivera to his closer spot. With the league's lowest ERA (3.84), fewest homers allowed (144) and best on-base percentage (.362), the Yankees won four more games than in '96 (96-66) to justify their untopped ($73 million) payroll. Most of the usual suspects — everyday players Bernie Williams, Paul O'Neill, Tino Martinez and Derek Jeter, pitchers Andy Pettitte, David Cone and Mariano Rivera — had their usual fine seasons. What fun the team had! With the start of inter-league play, the Yankees enjoyed games against the cross-town Mets and their '96 Series rivals, the Atlanta Braves. In an international coup, they signed Japanese pitching star Hideki Irabu to a four-year, $12.8 million contract.

A boisterous presence in an otherwise calm clubhouse, Wells, for one, was giddy. He took the mound against the Indians sporting a hat Babe Ruth once wore that Wells paid $35,000 for. Wells pitched with it for half an inning, then acceded to manager Joe Torre's demand and removed it to conform with major-league regulations. He surrendered eight hits and four runs before losing 12-8.

And that game proved to be a metaphor for the season. Irabu was 5-4 with a 7.09 ERA. Overall, the Yankees were great — the best team money could buy — but others were better. The Orioles led all season and won the division by two games over the wild-card Yankees. Then New York ran headlong into Cleveland. The divisional series started predictably at Yankee Stadium, with the Yankees getting three consecutive homers after trailing 6-1 and winning 8-6. The Indians took game two, 7-5. When play shifted to Cleveland's Jacobs Field, the Yanks won, 6-1, on Wells's fine pitching and Martinez's grand slam, and Yankee fans were ready to celebrate by the eighth inning of game four. They led, 2-1, and Rivera, who had transitioned superbly to his closer role, was on the mound. Whereupon Cleveland's Sandy Alomar, Jr., homered to tie the game. Even more surprising, shortstop Omar Vizquel, the ultimate glove man, drove home the winning run in the ninth with a grounder that glanced off the glove of reliever Ramiro Mendoza. In the winner-take-all fifth game Manny Ramirez, hitting .111 for the series, stroked a ground-rule double to give the Indians the 4-3 win. Afterward, Bob Watson resigned — the seventeenth general manager to go in the Steinbrenner era — and was replaced by former Yankee

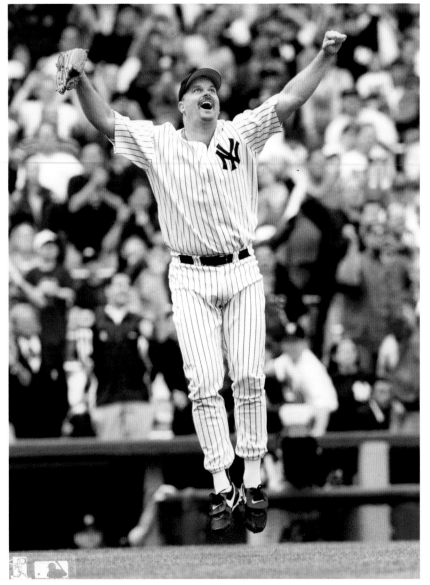

Below: *David Wells pitched a perfect game against the Twins in May of 1998 and kept rolling all season.*

intern Brian Cashman, who was all of 30. And old George was his everyday self, getting suspended from baseball's executive council for suing Major League Baseball over a sneaker deal.

Who'd have expected the 1998 Yankees to win a then-AL record 114 regular-season games and a record 125 overall? Cone was recovering from off-season shoulder surgery, Pettitte's arm had tired late in 1997 and some of the lineup changes—Scott Brosius for Charlie Hayes at third, Chili Davis, Tim Raines and Darryl Strawberry for Cecil Fielder at designated hitter —looked like so much flotsam-for-jetsam. When the Yankees lost their first three games Steinbrenner was already upset.

They recovered quickly to go 17-6 in April. The older Yankees in particular played like old-time Yankees. Cone, 35, would go 20-7 after a 10-year gap between 20-win seasons. No one in baseball history had waited longer. Wells blew up at Torre after being removed from a game earlier on May 6. But who could blame Torre? The fat man's ERA stood at a portly 5.77. Properly chastised, Wells turned his season around. Just 11 days later and shortly before his 35th birthday, he threw the second perfect game in Yankee history,

beating Minnesota 4-0. Afterward, comedian Billy Crystal approached Wells in the clubhouse. "I got here late," said Crystal, "what happened?"

What happened, Wells claimed (and later admitted he had exaggerated), was that he pitched the game hung over. Wells went 18-4, started the All-Star game, and walked only 16 batters in his final 170 1/3 innings. O'Neill, also 35, had the kind of season Yankee fans had grown to expect from him: a .317 average, 24 homers and 116 RBI. Plainly, some athletes are made for New York pressure. After arriving six seasons earlier with a .259 lifetime average, O'Neill had hit .317 in pinstripes. For his part, Bernie Williams, a New York sophisticate who plays classical guitar, hit a league-best .339 in his free-agent-eligible season. There were no genuine superstars on the '98 team, but long-time baseball watchers said they'd never seen so many great two-strike hitters. All of this more than atoned for the failure of new second baseman Chuck Knoblauch, a .300 hitter who dipped into the .260s.

The Yankees were unstoppable. After winning the regular season title, they swept the Rangers in the ALDS despite hearing the news that outfielder Strawberry had

Above: *David Cone replicated Wells's feat with a perfect game of his own against Montreal in 1999.*

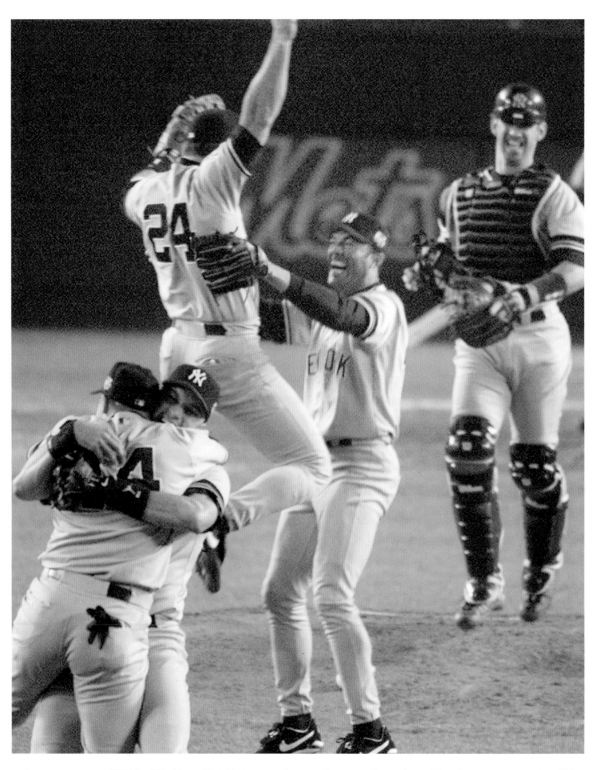

Above: *Amid a team celebration, Luis Soto (left) is hugged by Derek Jeter after driving in the deciding run of the 2000 World Series.*

colon cancer. With Wells, Pettitte and Cone getting the wins, the Yankees held off the tough Texans 2-0, 3-1 and 4-0. A two-run homer by Scott Brosius and a three-run shot by Shane Spencer gave them most of the offense they needed. In the ALCS opener, the Yanks beat the Indians 7-2, kayoing Jaret Wright after 36 pitches. After New York lost the second and third games, with second baseman Chuck Knoblauch contributing to one loss by arguing with an umpire while a run scored, Orlando (El Duque) Hernández, late of the Cuban national team, stopped Cleveland cold, 4-0, and New York won in six games.

The World Series started with the Padres ahead 5-2 after six innings. Then two under-performing Yankees came to life. Knoblauch homered to tie the score, and Martinez, who had one RBI in 76 previous ALCS and World Series at bats, hit a grand slam on a 3-and-2 pitch to put the game out of reach. El Duque throttled San Diego 9-3. Then the Yankees overcame another three-run deficit. MVP Brosius stroked a three-run homer on a 3-and-2 pitch from Trevor Hoffman, who had secured 53 of 54 save opportunities during the season, capping a 5-4 win in game three. Pettitte won his first start in 10 days, 3-0, the runs scoring on a groundout, a blooper and a sacrifice fly, in the finale of the World Series four-game sweep. And who could forget leftfielder Ricky Ledee, little-used inseason, who went 6-for-10, with four RBI?

The 1998 team looked every bit the equal of the legendary 1927 and 1939 Yanks.

How do you replicate perfection in the 1999 season? By trading a heartbroken Wells to Toronto for Roger Clemens, who had just won two Cy Young Awards and convinced doubters that he may be the greatest pitcher in baseball history. And by taking the word "perfect" literally.

On July 18, the old Yankee catcher and manager Yogi Berra and Steinbrenner ended their long dispute with a day in Yogi's honor. Yogi stood behind the plate and Don Larsen, who pitched a perfect game in the 1956 World Series, threw the first ball to him. Then they sat back and watched Cone play Larsen.

Cone retired the first six men. Despite a 33-minute rain delay in the third inning, he continued blanking the Expos through the fourth and fifth. At that point, he said later, he realized he had a no-hitter going.

Equally aware of the Expos' free-swinging habits, he located one slider after another just out of the strike zone and struck out 10 batters. In the eighth inning, Knoblauch of all people made a fine backhand stop and a great throw to rob Jose Vidro of a hit. On the final out, Orlando Cabrera popped to third baseman Scott Brosius, whereupon Cone fell to his knees and hugged catcher Joe Girardi. All in all, a magical day for another magic man with magic hands. As Berra himself might have put it, "Déjà vu all over again."

Despite more torment for Torre, who missed the first month and a half for prostate-cancer surgery (Don Zimmer filled in as manager), the 1999 Yankees won 98 games and their second straight divisional title. They swept the Rangers—limiting them to one run again—then faced the Red Sox for the first time in the postseason, courtesy of the new wild-card

Below: *A key mid-season acquisition, outfielder/designated hitter David Justice homers in the 2000 Fall Classic.*

arrangement. Though the Yankees beat the Red Sox in five, the ALDS was reminiscent of many other memorable Boston-New York dust-ups. The Yankees tied the opener on Jeter's single, which scored Scott Brosius when he kicked the ball out of catcher Jason Varitek's glove. Bernie Williams's walk-off homer won the game in the tenth. The Sox also led game two before two-out hits by Knoblauch and O'Neill won it in the seventh, 3-2. Boston took some revenge by beating ex-Sox Clemens, 13-1, but the Yankees returned from behind to win game four, 9-2, and MVP Hernández and four relievers ended the series, 6-1. Umpires blew three calls that would have helped the Red Sox, and outraged Boston fans littered the field in the finale. In short, it was business as usual between the Sox and the Yanks.

If a World Series can be anticlimactic, the 1999 version was. With MVP Rivera getting two saves and a win and Leyritz fittingly driving in the last run with a homer, the Yankees swept the Braves for their second title in three years. El Duque was his

usual masterful self in game one, which he won, 4-1, after allowing one hit in seven innings. Cone pitched another beauty and won, 7-2, before things finally heated up. The Braves got 14 hits and knocked out Pettitte after 3 2/3 innings of game three, but the Yankees rallied to tie the game, 5-5, when Knoblauch's drive tipped off Brian Jordan's glove for a homer. Another four-bagger, this one by leftfielder Chad Curtis, won the game, 6-5, in 10 innings. Before game four O'Neill learned that his father had died. He played anyway, and the Yankees ended the Series, 4-1, behind Clemens's pitching. Rivera now had a streak of six saves, two wins and no runs allowed in the postseason. In case you weren't counting, the Yankees went 11-1 this particular October. Their 12-win streak in the Series play tied their own record, and they completed back-to-back sweeps in the World Series for the first time since, yes, the Yankees did it in 1938-9.

For a while the Yankees struggled in 2000. In fact, if they hadn't acquired slugger David Justice in-season—Kid Cash-

Below: *Twice a Yankee, Cuban pitcher Orlando (El Duque) Hernández won his first eight postseason decisions.*

man was named Executive of the Year for the move—the Yankees might not have won 87 games and another divisional title. As it was, they lost 15 of their last 18 games and entered the postseason with the worst record of the eight qualifiers. They beat Oakland in a five-game division series, but barely. Both teams had to fly overnight to Oakland for the finale, a 7-5 squeaker manned by starter Pettitte and four exhausted relievers, Mike Stanton getting the win.

Having won the ALDS, the Yanks were shut out for the first 16 innings of the ALCS by Seattle before a seven-run eighth in game two set things right. After tying the series at one game apiece, the Yan-

kees won twice—game four on a nifty Clemens one-hitter—before losing game five. No problem: An upper-deck shot by MVP Justice won game six, 9-7, and sent the Yankees to the first Subway Series in 44 years, this time against the Mets. El Duque, game two winner as a starter and game six winner in relief, was now 8-0 in postseason play.

Though the Yankees won in five, the Series was well contested. With the Mets leading game one, 4-3, the slumping O'Neill fouled off four two-strike pitches before walking to start a ninth-inning rally in which Knoblauch's sacrifice fly sent the contest into extra innings. Jose Vizcaino's run-scoring single won it 4-3 for the Yanks

Above: *Scott Brosius was Series MVP in 1998, but his fielding misjudgment cost the Yankees in 2001.*

Above: *Mike Mussina, a Yankee since 2001, chose to retire in 2008 after finishing with his first 20-win season.*

in the twelfth. They won their fourteenth straight Series game the next day after some especially dramatic touches. There was bad blood between the Yanks and Mets dating back to an in-season game in which Clemens hit Mets catcher Mike Piazza on the head, giving him a concussion. Piazza said it was a purpose pitch. In the first inning of the Series, Piazza shattered his bat on a foul ball and started running to first. Clemens fielded a remnant and threw it toward the first-base dugout but uncomfortably close to Piazza, emptying both benches. Clemens was later fined $50,000.

Keeping his cool this time, Piazza said that Clemens "seemed extremely apologetic and unsure and confused and unstable" on the field. If so, Clemens settled down, allowing two hits over eight innings as the Yankees took a 6-0 lead. The Mets' five-run ninth fell short. Snapping Rivera's postseason record of 34 1/3 consecutive scoreless innings and giving Hernández his first postseason loss, the Mets won game three, 4-2. MVP Jeter's leadoff homer set the standard for a Yankee win in game four, although a managerial move contributed. Torre replaced starter Denny Neagle with two outs and no one on and the Yankees leading 3-2 in the fifth, summoning Cone to retire the dangerous Piazza on a popup. The Yankees and their bullpen hung on to win 3-2, with Jeff Nelson getting the victory. In game five, Luis Sojo's single in the ninth wrapped up another Fall Classic, the Yankees' fourth title in five years, at a final score of 4-2, with another unheralded set-up man, Mike Stanton, getting the decision. Yes, another Yankee dynasty

had been certified. Not since the 1972-4 Oakland A's had a team won three or more consecutive World Series.

At this point, it would have been hard to find a more popular figure in New York City than Joe Torre. To be sure, he had some built-in advantages. Italian-American, born and bred in Brooklyn, a Regular Joe in temperament, he was a natural fan favorite. He'd inherited the makings of a championship team from Buck Showalter. But Torre was also living the ultimate American Dream, one anybody could relate to. He was winning despite having Steinbrenner for a boss.

Who'd have thought the dynasty would end so abruptly, and so miserably? In 2001, the extraordinary Clemens went 20-3 to win the Cy Young Award and the Yankees took their fourth straight division title, grabbing a 95-65 record in a season delayed by the 9/11 attacks. But these weren't your father's Yankees. Or were they?

The Yankees were down two games to none and facing elimination in the ALDS, when Mike Mussina nursed a one-run lead over the A's. With Jeremy Giambi edging off first, Oakland rightfielder Terrence Long rifled a shot into the right-field corner. As Giambi rounded third, Yankee rightfielder Shane Spencer overthrew the cutoff man and the ball rolled down the first-base line. Giambi was running home with no intention of sliding. Somehow, Jeter raced from his shortstop position, grabbed the ball and flipped backhanded to catcher Jorge Posada, who applied the tag on Giambi. What looked like a tie game on the edge of disaster became a Yankee win, followed by two more and the division title. Jeter's play, voted seventh best of all time by "Baseball America," was real "Pride of the Yankees" stuff, something Yankee fans had seen a lot of in recent years. O'Neill's limping grab, Torre's courage, Jeter's heads-up play: No wonder the Yankees looked like perennial champions. No wonder old fans were conjuring up Babe, Lou, Joe, Mickey and Reggie.

Alas, reality turned Golden Pond into Dismal Swamp. The Yankees needed five games to get by Seattle in the ALCS. Then came a rock-'em, sock-'em seven-game World Series against Arizona that started late on October 27. Everyone assumed the Yankees, sentimental favorites due to the 9/11 attacks and practical favorites because they were, well, the Yankees, would win. Arizona pitcher Curt Schilling begged to differ. "Mystique and aura?" he said. "They're dancers at a nightclub."

The Yankees and Diamondbacks split the first six games, including one in which Jeter hit a walk-off homer just after midnight to earn the nickname Mr. November. It all came down to the ninth inning of game seven: What else? The Yankees were leading 2-1, Mariano Rivera was on the mound, and all seemed right with the world since he'd converted his last 23 postseason save attempts. Mark Grace reached on a single, and David Dellucci ran for him. Damian Miller laid down a poor bunt. Rivera fielded it quickly, but his throw to second was errant. Suddenly, the Diamondbacks had men on first and second with none out. Pinch-hitting for pitcher Randy Johnson, Jay Bell also bunted, and this time Rivera's throw to third baseman Scott Brosius came in time for the force. Unfortunately, Brosius didn't notice that Bell was still far from first and failed to relay there for a double play. Rattled, Rivera gave up a game-tying double to Tony Womack on what some stat hounds called the best clutch hit ever. Craig Counsell was hit by a pitch to load the bases, bringing the infield in, and Luis Gonzalez's bloop just past second base scored a run that decided the first Series to end in November.

Afterward, Rivera blamed Brosius for his nonexistent relay. Others blamed Rivera for his poor throw to second. A Series ending amid turmoil didn't augur well for another Yankee dynasty.

Below: *Shortstop Derek Jeter tumbles into the stands after catching a foul ball in one of his typical all-out efforts that enhanced his reputation and endeared him to the fans.*

11. Heartaches By the Number

Above: *Japanese import Hideki Matsui (center), a dependable leftfielder, is congratulated after a game-winning run.*

The 2002 Yankees were down but hardly out. In fact, they spoke as one. When the club cut journeyman outfielder Ruben Rivera for allegedly stealing Derek Jeter's glove to sell as memorabilia, everyone in the clubhouse applauded his ouster. Of more consequence, the Yankees signed Oakland first baseman/designated hitter Jason Giambi, and he responded by batting .314, with 41 homers and 122 RBI. Even more eye-catching was young second baseman Alfonso Soriano, who nearly had a rare 40-homer, 40-steal season. Roger Clemens lost the season opener, but Yankee pitchers authored shutouts in the next three games. With David Wells winning 19 games and Mike Mussina 18, the Yanks moved into first place on June 28 and won their fifth straight division title by 10 1/2 games over Boston with the season's best (103-58) record. Not even an off-year by the ailing Rivera, who had only 28 saves, could stall the Yankee express, which steamed into the postseason favored against the wild-card Angels in the ALDS.

And then the pitching ran out of gas. The Yankees got by the first game, winning, 8-5, on Bernie Williams's three-run homer in the eighth, but they had no answers when starters Andy Pettitte (three innings), Mussina (four) and Wells (4 2/3) came up short in the next three games. As they lost the finale after building up a 6-1 lead, the team's earned-run average ballooned to 10.39 and the Yankees missed the World Series for the first time since 1997.

In 2003, the Yankees led the division from June 12 on and captured their sixth straight division title with a 101-61 record. As usual, they won the battle of headlines, in this case by outbidding everyone else for Japanese outfielder Hideki Matsui. As a result, it was hard to find a hole in the New York attack, with Matsui (106 RBI), Giambi (41 homers, 107 RBI, .412 on-base percentage), Soriano (38 HR, 91 RBI), Posada (30 HR, 91 RBI) and Jeter (.324 average) among the league leaders. The pitching was deep and strong with Pettitte (21 wins), Clemens (17), Mussina (17), Wells (15) and Rivera (40 saves). Clemens won his 300th game and joined Nolan Ryan and Steve Carlton in the 4,000-strikeout club. The season's only embarrassment came on June 11, when six Astro pitchers combined to no-hit

Below: *Roger Clemens, certainly one of the best pitchers in baseball history, starred for the Yankees in 1999-2003, then returned in 2007 before retiring. Unfortunately his reputation has been tarnished by charges of using drugs, charges that he denied even to the point of going to trial in 2011.*

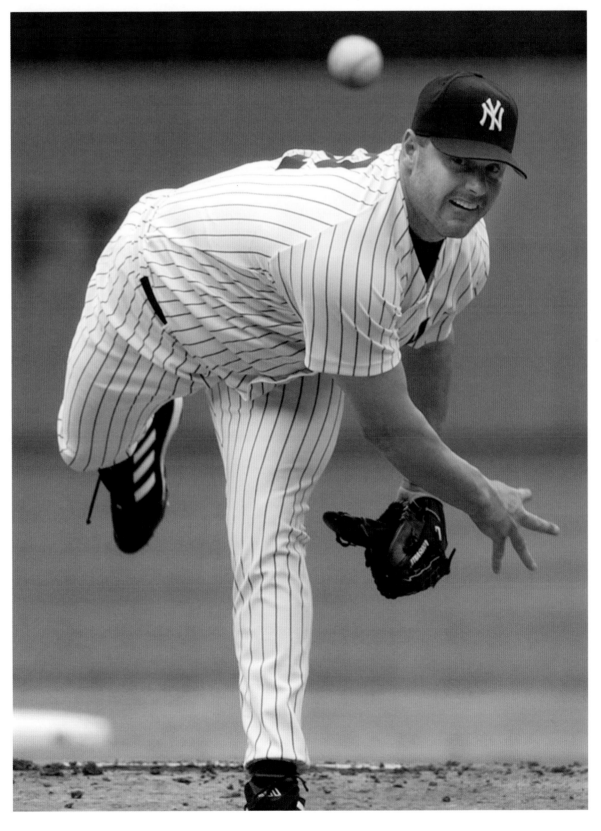

the Yankees, 8-0. And yet, the Yankees would fall short of the one goal they have with every season.

They lost once to the Twins before winning the ALDS in four, with Wells, Pettitte, Clemens and their relievers holding the Twins to six runs. Scuffling to win the ALCS, they lost composure during game three against the Red Sox. It had been a typically nasty game, with Clemens plunking Karim Garcia on the back and Garcia sliding hard into second baseman Todd Walker. When Clemens threw high but not particularly tight to Manny Ramirez in the third inning, Ramirez began walking toward the mound, bat in hand, and both benches emptied. Pretty standard stuff so far, until Yankee bench coach Don Zimmer suddenly charged at Pedro Martinez, who was standing near the Yankee dugout. Martinez promptly threw Zimmer to the ground, and Zimmer subsequently said he was "embarrassed" by his own behavior. In the ninth inning, two Yankees fought a Red Sox employee in the bullpen. The omnipresent Garcia and Jeff Nelson later reached a plea agreement giving them six months' probation and 50 hours of community service, while charges were dropped against the employee. Thus did the Yankees enter Miss Manners' book for poor comportment.

After the first six games were split, the Red Sox led game seven, 5-2, going into the eighth. Happily for the Yanks, Red Sox manager Grady Little left a tiring Martinez on the hill after 122 pitches, and the Yankees tied the score with four straight hits. MVP Rivera pitched three scoreless innings before the Yanks' Aar-

Below: Yankee coach Don Zimmer charged Boston pitcher Pedro Martinez and was thrown to the ground in the 2003 postseason.

on Boone hit a walk-off homer against Tim Wakefield in the eleventh. Yanks 6, Boston 5. Whew!

There was no fighting their way out of the Series though. Because the American League had won the All-Star game, the newly adopted rule meant that the Fall Classic started in New York, where the young Florida Marlins and their 72-year-old manager Jack McKeon were anything but intimidated by the monuments, the history and the Yankees' $105 million payroll advantage. The Fish got their first run on a drag bunt, a single and a sacrifice fly, and they went on to win the opener, 3-2. The Yankees won the next two while Bernie Williams hit a postseason record nineteenth homer, but when Clemens staged what was ballyhooed as potentially his last major-league start, the Marlins won game four on Alex Gonzalez's leadoff homer in the twelfth. Age and experience, bah! Wells left game five with back spasms from a chronic lower-back injury, more than enough incentive for the Marlins to win, 6-4. And 23-year-old Josh Beckett, pitching on three days' rest, shut out the Yankees, 2-0, to win the Series. In the aftermath, Zimmer retired, and the Yankees fired pitching coach Rick Downs as the whipping boy for Giambi and Soriano slumps and injuries in the Series. It was emblematic of the lost season that an error by Jeter — his first in 27 Series games — contributed to the Series-ending loss.

With only 12 players back from the 2003 roster on Opening Day 2004, the new-look Yanks no longer had Clemens, Pettitte, Soriano or Wells and relied on newcomers like pitchers Kevin Brown, Javier Vázquez and Orlando Hernández (back for his second Yankee stint). They did get reigning MVP Alex (A-Rod) Rodriguez from Texas for Soriano, but Giambi arrived in camp thinner than usual, suffered mysterious ailments, admitted steroid use and hit .208 in just 80 games.

The Yankees opened in the Tokyo Dome on March 30 and lost, 8-3, to Tampa Bay. By October, New York was 101-61 but won the division by only three games over Boston, with no regular hitting over .300, no pitcher winning 15 games, and Rivera's league-leading 53 saves keeping them in first. Who'd have expected the likes of Vázquez and Jon Lieber to head the staff with 14 wins each? Who'd have thought the Yankees would need old Gary Sheffield, who finished second in the MVP balloting with 117 runs, 36 homers and 121 RBI? Especially disappointing was Rodriguez. Although the best all-around shortstop in baseball, he moved to third rather than displace Mr. New York, Derek Jeter. He had a most un-A-Rod season—if an excellent year for anyone else—batting .286, with 36 homers, 106 RBI and 28 stolen bases.

On July 1, 2004, Jeter at least played true to form. With the score tied 3-3, the bases loaded and two outs in the twelfth against archrival Boston, Red Sox rightfielder Trot Nixon hit what appeared to be a perfectly placed pop fly down the left-field line. Everyone expected that it would drop between third baseman Rodriguez and leftfielder Ruben Sierra. Out of nowhere, Jeter made an over-the-shoulder catch. Momentum sent him diving into the stands, from which he emerged with a bloody face and the ball. The Yankees won in the thirteenth to complete a three-game sweep.

A-Rod hit .421 and scored the decisive run in the four-game ALDS win against Minnesota. He began respectably when the Yanks swept the first three games of the ALCS against Boston. The Yankees led game four, 4-3, with Rivera on the mound in the ninth inning. Then he committed the cardinal sin of pitching by walking the leadoff man, Kevin Millar. Dave Roberts pinch ran, everyone knew he would try to steal second, and he just beat Posada's throw, which was a smidgeon off. Bill Mueller singled him in, and the game went into extra innings on Rivera's fourth blown save in 36 postseason appearances. Although

the Yankees put men on base in the next three, ever tenser innings, none scored, and Boston's David Ortiz won the game with a twelfth inning homer. The Red Sox won game five, 5-4, in 14, Ortiz doing the job this time with a broken-bat single, and took the series to a maximum seven when Curt Schilling, with his ankle bloodied from a dislocated tendon, won game six, 4-2. And suddenly the light went out of the Yankee season. Johnny Damon's grand slam put New York away early, and the Red Sox won game seven, 10-3.

No one in baseball history had trailed a postseason series three games to none and won it. Boston fans, therefore, celebrated an unprecedented comeback, while Yankee supporters lamented a historic collapse. Who better to blame than A-Rod, who went 2-for-17 in the final four games?

The 2005 Yankees opened at Fenway Park and beat the world champion Red Sox, 9-2, with Randy Johnson (17-8, 211 strikeouts) getting the win in his Yankee debut. Despite a failed $61 million investment in Carl Pavano and Jaret Wright, the rotation kept getting better and better. Chien-Ming Wang of Taiwan gave up two runs over seven innings in his major-league debut, a 4-3 win over Los Angeles. Journeyman pitcher Aaron Small (10-0) was only the fourth player with at least 10 wins to go unbeaten, veteran Al Leiter pitched well in an emer-

Above: *Aaron Boone broke Red Sox hearts with an eleventh-inning homer that sent the Yankees to the 2003 World Series.*

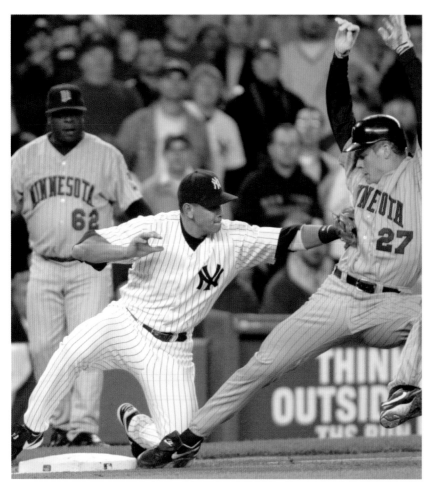

Above: *Alex Rodriguez tagged out the Twins' Justin Morneau in the 2004 ALCS, but his bat failed in postseason play.*

gency start and Rivera had his usual 43 saves. Criticized for inconsistent fielding in the past, Jeter won a Gold Glove.

Rodriguez became the youngest player (29 years, 316 days) to hit his 400th homer, had a 10-RBI game, led the league in homers (48), slugging (.610) and runs (124) and became the first Yankee MVP since Don Mattingly in 1985. Comeback Player of the Year Giambi had 32 homers, 87 RBI and a league-best 108 walks. In a test of mettle on September 16, rookie Robinson Cano hit two homers to help the Yankees build up an 11-3 lead at Toronto that they almost blew before winning, 11-10.

After trailing the Red Sox most of the way, the Yankees clinched first place on the penultimate day of the season and finished with a 95-67 record for their ninth straight divisional title. (The Red Sox finished with an identical record, but New York was awarded first place because of its 10-9 advantage in head-to-head play.) When you're expected to win it all, the season is just an appetizer. How they performed in the postseason would define the 2005 Yankees.

In the division series, the Yankees split four games with Los Angeles. The decisive fifth game couldn't have started better. L.A. starter Bartolo Colon left the game in the second inning with an arm injury and was replaced by 22-year-old rookie Ervin Santana, who promptly

surrendered two runs. Which one would you take: Santana or 224-game winning veteran Mike Mussina? Yankee fans quickly learned which, to their horror. Santana only gave up one more run in the next 4 1/3 innings, while Mussina was rocked for five in the second and third. The go-ahead run scored when outfielders Sheffield and Bubba Crosby collided on what looked like an easy fly to right-center. With relief help from Kelvim Escobar and Francisco Rodriguez, Santana got the 5-3 win and the Yankees slumped home. It was the second straight year the Angels beat the Yankees in the first round.

Uncrowned in the last five postseasons, the Yankees invited endless hot-stove post-mortems. It scarcely helped that they put three men on base without scoring in their final inning. Inevitably, critics searched for a scapegoat, and once again no one loomed larger than A-Rod, who grounded into a double play in the ninth and hit .133, with no homers or RBI, in the series. A complicated man who announced he was in therapy and took a tour of the Harvard campus when the Yankees were in Boston, Rodriguez constantly seeks self-knowledge. The question Yankee fans started asking was if the New York City fishbowl was the best place for him to find it.

With Ron Guidry installed as the new pitching coach, the 2006 Yankees (97-65) still won their customary divisional title, but attention focused elsewhere. Who could concentrate on Jeter and Johnson when the Detroit Tigers, losers of 119 games just three seasons earlier, led the AL Central until the final days and won an unexpected wild-card spot in the postseason? And how easy was it to admire the level-headed Torre when Detroit's intense, chain-smoking Jim Leyland was a cinch for Manager of the Year? Even fine pitching from Wang (19-6) and production from Rodriguez and Giambi in the absence of the disabled Sheffield and Matsui passed little-noted outside of New York. Jeter's best season (.343, 118 runs, 214 hits, Gold Glove) earned him only a second-place finish in MVP voting.

There was, moreover, unsettling news about A-Rod. His fielding grew erratic, his hitting spotty. In September, *Sports Illustrated* reported an exchange between him and Giambi in which Giambi demanded that he get more big hits. A-Rod scarcely helped himself when he told *Sports Illustrated*, "[Mike] Mussina doesn't get hammered at all. He's making a boatload of money. Giambi's making [$20.4 million], which is fine and dandy, but it seems those guys get a pass. When people write [bad things] about me, I don't know if it's [because] I'm good-looking, I'm biracial, I make the most money, I play on the most popular team..." The statement left the unsettling impression that A-Rod was more concerned about his *GQ* image than his play.

Well, the Yankees thought they would surely set things straight in the ALDS when they faced the upstart Tigers. Wang won the opener, 8-4, while Jeter went 5-for-5, and the Yankees built up a 3-1 lead in game two on Johnny Damon's three-run, third-inning homer. Who knew the Yankees wouldn't score again for two games? The Tigers fought back and won, 4-3, on Curtis Granderson's ninth-inning triple. Then 41-year-old Kenny Rogers threw 7 2/3 scoreless innings to win game three, 6-0, in the Tigers' first postseason home game since 1987. And the fans at Comerica Park stood as one when their Jeremy Bonderman closed out the series by beating Jaret Wright, 8-3.

New York's post-mortem waxed long and grim. The easy target, yet again, was A-Rod, who went 1-for-14 against Detroit and batted eighth in the final game. He insisted he wanted to remain in Gotham. Meanwhile, a mellower George Steinbrenner re-upped with Torre rather than blame his skipper for failing to motivate A-Rod. But these developments were buried in the gloom of other news. Pitcher Cory Lidle died in a plane crash. The Red Sox outbid the Yankees for the rights to negotiate with Japanese pitcher Daisuke Matsuzaka, widely equated with the best in the majors. Randy Johnson underwent back surgery. The Yankees fought back by re-signing Pettitte and bidding $33 million for the rights to negotiate with lefthander

Kei Igawa, a likely third or fourth pitcher in the rotation.

Busy as ever when the trading season began, the Yankees sent Sheffield to Detroit for three young pitchers and shipped Wright to Baltimore for reliever Chris Britton. But the Sheffield move took a righthanded bat out of the lineup, putting more pressure on A-Rod. In an era of instant gratification, the Yankees have gone six years without a world championship. Certainly there have been periods of drought in Yankee history like 1965-75 and 1982-93. And the Steinbrenner era had seen accomplishment followed by retrenchment before. The majority owner built up the team in the seventies before tearing it down in the eighties. Joe Torre restored Yankee luster in 1996-2000, and for all the attendant frustration, the 2001-6 Yankees have reached the postseason every time. If only A-Rod could produce in October.

The Yankees were literally blindsided in 2007. True, they weren't expected to win the division after the Red Sox signed Japanese hurler Daisuke Matsuzaka. True, they would grab a wild-card playoff spot by finishing second to Boston with a 94-86 record, bolstered by A-Rod's MVP season (.314, 54 homers, 156 RBI) and Chien-Ming Wang's 19-7 pitching. But what happened afterward left an indelible stain.

First, though, they had to get to the playoffs. Having traded Gary Sheffield to the Tigers for several prospects, short-circuiting the team's righthanded hitting behind Rodriguez, the Yankees staggered through the spring to a 21-29 last-place start and by May 29 trailed the first-place Red Sox by 14 1/2 games. The day before, Torre, normally the pattern of all patience, lashed into

Below: *Jason Giambi joined the Yankees in 2002. Although a solid hitter and first baseman, medical problems restricted his hoped-for contributions to the team and in 2009 he joined the Rockies.*

Above: *Johnny Damon joined the Yankees in 2006 and proved to be a reliable hitter. In 2010 he joined the Detroit Tigers, but in 2011 he showed up as the DH with the Tampa Bay Rays.*

Right: *Joba Chamberlain had to fight an infestation of midges when he was called in for relief in game two of the ALDS against Cleveland.*

Opposite: *Alex Rodriguez's 2007 season earned him the MVP.*

the team's tentative play. Good grief, the players whispered to each other, we've never seen old Joe so mad.

The tongue-lashing must have worked, because after the All-Star break the Yankees had the majors' best record (51-29). Key to their resurgence were Melky Cabrera claiming the center-field job; the lefthanded hitting of Bobby Abreu, Robinson Cano and Hideki Matsui; and the switch-hitting of leftfielder Johnny Damon. Righthanded reliever Joba Chamberlain, who began the season at A-ball Tampa, was promoted in August to the big club, where he yielded a single run and no wild pitches, fanned 34 batters over 24 innings, compiled a 0.53 ERA and sent fans into spasms of joy over their rejuvenated short-relief corps.

Ah, but the Yankees still had to face the mighty Cleveland Indians and their secret stadium scourge in the American League Division Series. The Indians beat Wang, 3-1, to take the opener at Jacobs Field. With the Yankees leading game two, 1-0, in the eighth inning, Chamberlain came undone when Lake Erie bugs called midges invaded his eyes, mouth and nostrils. After walking leadoff hitter Grady Sizemore, the partially blinded Chamberlain wild-pitched him to second. With midges on his neck and swarming around his face, Chamberlain applied more bug spray. But after Cabrera sacrificed Sizemore to third and Travis Hafner lined to first for the second out, Chamberlain uncorked another wild pitch to score Sizemore, prompting ESPN. com's Jason Stark to ask, "So where was the Sultan of Swat when the Yankees really needed him?"

The Indians won the game, 2-1, with a run in the eleventh. New York's Roger Clemens, 45, who had drifted out of retirement for possibly the last time and gone 6-6 with a 4.18 ERA while making $17 million, left after just 2 1/3 innings of an 8-4 New York win at Yankee Stadium in game three. Whereupon in game four the Indians beat Wang again, this time 6-4, to eliminate the Yankees in the first round for the third year running. The game was nowhere near as close as it sounds. The Indians led, 6-1 after 3 1/2 innings, leaving 56,315 stadium fans to spend the rest of the game contemplating the detritus of the Yankee year. A-Rod homered in the seventh, little noted nor long remembered. Forever slighted around Gotham for his postseason failures, he didn't get a hit until the Yankees trailed, two games to none.

The offseason began when longtime good sailors started edging toward the glistening waters of free agency. Among them were catcher Jorge Posada, who

Above: *After his great 2007 season Derek Jeter's stats declined a bit in 2008, but in 2009 he returned to form with 212 hits and a .334 BA.*

had one of his best (.338, 20 homers, 90 RBI) seasons, and closer Mariano Rivera, who suffered one of his worst (30 saves, two blown saves to Red Sox in 24 hours, 3.15 ERA). Torre, offered an insulting contract extension, left for the Dodgers; Mattingly joined him as special assignments coach. Torre was replaced by former Yankee Joe Girardi,

who had been National League Manager of the Year with the 2006 Florida Marlins. In what looked like the crowning blow, A-Rod's agent announced during game four of the World Series that his client was opting out of his contract.

Posada and Rivera eventually re-upped with the Yankees, and A-Rod dumped his agent, negotiated with the team himself after a consultation with billionaire Warren Buffett, and signed a record 10-year, $275 million extension with them. "By speaking out, A-Rod showed that beneath his robotic exterior lurks a real player and a real human, one who values 'comfort, stability, and happiness,' as he put it in a message on his Web site," Bryan Curtis wrote in Slate.com.

The good feelings wouldn't last for long. As the year ran out, David Szen, who had been the team's public relations director and traveling secretary over a 25-year career, pleaded guilty to filing a false income tax return and owing the government $10,285. He heard about his firing over the Internet. Even that embarrassment took a back seat to the 311-page Mitchell Report on performance-enhancing drugs in the major leagues that was released on December 13. Ten Yankees from the 2000 team were cited as users before, during and after the season, including Clemens and lefthander Andy Pettitte. Both were said to have been supplied by former Yankee strength coach Brian McNamee. Clemens's credibility took a beating when his friend and training partner Pettitte confirmed McNamee's finding and admitted to twice using Human Growth Hormone (HGH) to rehab an injury in 2002.

Although he was mentioned on eight pages of the report, Clemens loudly protested his innocence through spokesmen, on a video, in an interview with Mike Wallace on "60 Minutes" and at a press conference. Clemens's claim that McNamee had injected him with neither steroids nor HGH but with B-12 and the painkiller lidocaine had people rolling their eyes. Among many critics, *Sports Illustrated*'s Richard Hoffer wrote that "doctors...find it strange that a trainer would administer a prescription drug like lidocaine or that anybody needs to inject B-12. That, by the way, has become one very notorious vitamin; Rafael Palmeiro said he was mistakenly dosed with steroids during a routine B-12 shot. The question remains: Can't anybody just grab a fistful of Flintstones and be done with it?"

Clemens scarcely improved his image at a bizarre press conference when he was asked if the allegations would hurt his chances to make the Hall of Fame. His reply that he "could give a rat's ass" about the shrine was not only vulgar but unbelievable.

But if the Yankees were down, they could not be counted out, at least not just yet. Great things were anticipated from Chamberlain, who was expected to join the rotation in 2008, and promising youngsters Phil Hughes (5-3, 58 strikeouts in 77 2/3 innings) and Ian Kennedy

(1-0, 15 K's in 19 innings, 1.89 ERA) could atone for any continued drop-off by aging Mike Mussina (11-10, 5.15 ERA). Lest we forget, the everyday players did lead the majors with 968 runs, and the team may be run more coherently now that George Steinbrenner's son Hank has succeeded him at the helm. When Girardi was introduced as manager, he said: "This is the New York Yankees. This is a stable organization. It's not going anywhere, and it's going to be here long after we're gone."

Above: *Jorge Posada was an invaluable contributor to the Yankees for 15 seasons as both catcher and hitter. Injuries cut short his 2008 season but in 2009 he returned with a respectable .363 on-base percentage.*

Below: *Joe Girardi, who caught for the Yankees in 1996-1999, became their new manager after the end of the 2007 season.*

Right: *Because of an injury in 2008, Hideki Matsui did not have his usual productive season at the plate. In 2009 as DH he returned to form and was named MVP of the World Series, but he joined the Angels in 2010.*

Below: *Mariano Rivera had two of his better seasons in 2008 and 2009, with a combined 83 saves and an average 1.58 ERA. He also threw the last pitch in the old Yankees Stadium.*

The 2008 Yankees felt so confident that they made only marginal changes to the roster. All during the off-season, the Steinbrenners pointedly abstained from the bidding for free-agent Johan Santana, a southpaw who eventually signed with the Mets and 16-7 with a 2.53 ERA. The club will do just fine, officials said, with Kennedy and Hughes. The club looked forward, moreover, to a historic season, the last to be played at the old Yankee Stadium. Major League Baseball wisely assigned the All-Star Game to the shrine but strangely scheduled the final game there on September 21 rather than the last day of the season. No matter. As the most successful team in pro sports history, the Yankees could only end their 83-year stay at the stadium in style.

That was the script, but from the beginning it wasn't followed. Kennedy, Hughes and young call-up Darrell Rasner went 11-21. There was precious little leadership from veteran pitchers. The team lost Chien-Ming Wang (8-2) to a fluke leg injury while he was rounding the bases, and Pettitte

stumbled to a 14-14 record and a 4.54 earned run average after confirming the Mitchell Report finding that he had used human growth hormone. Joba Chamberlain made his much-anticipated shift from bullpen to rotation, got hurt and pitched only 100 1/3 innings. It didn't help that excellent defensive catcher Jorge Posada was disabled and reduced to 51 games. Not even a mid-season trade with Detroit that landed future Hall-of-Fame catcher Iván Rodriguez could bail out the sorry staff. Another sterling year from closer Rivera, who had 39 saves and a 1.40 ERA, kept the Yanks from dropping out even earlier. He looked like a bargain at three years for $45 million.

Nor was there much help on offense. Left-fielder Hideki Matsui got banged up, played half a season and accumulated about half his usual output with 9 homers and 45 RBI. The much-touted Melky Cabrera was an embarrassment. A-Rod, Derek Jeter and Bobby Abreu had decent numbers, but the Yankees finished with 789 runs, well down from 968 the previous season and seventh in the league. While the lads were losing a home game against the Red Sox, A-Rod came to the plate in a moment that personified the season. Never popular at Yankee Stadium, constantly cited as a poor clutch hitter, he was now being sued for divorce on grounds of adultery — possibly involving the singer/actress Madonna. A tabloid headline called him "Stray-Rod." The boos rained down on him. After grounding into two double plays — one with the bases loaded — Rodriguez struck out to end the game.

With the Yankees 64-57 on August 14 and 10 games behind front-running Tampa Bay, blogger Bill Chuck wrote: "Every year since 1995 when October came around you could ask the question, 'When's the Yan-

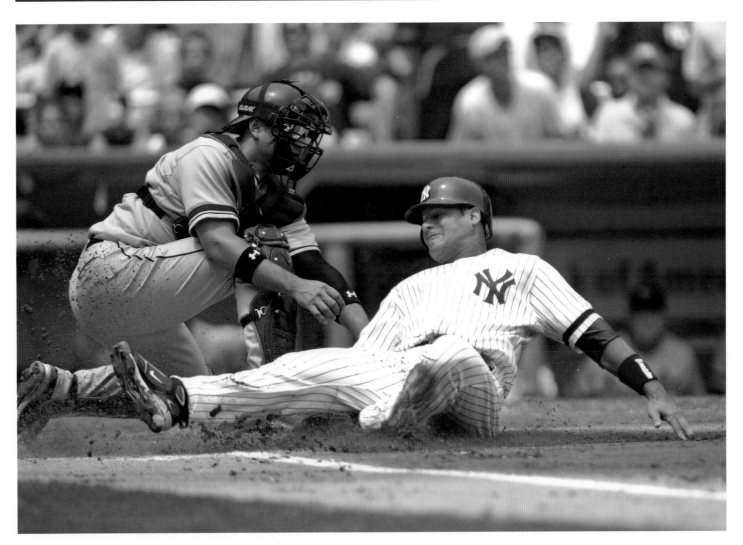

kees' first post-season game?' This year the Yanks and their fans will have to provide the answer of the old Brooklyn Dodgers, 'Wait 'til next year.' For those of you who revel in Yankee schadenfreude, you can plan two parties this year, one when they are eliminated from the Divisional race and the second when they are eliminated from the Wild Card race."

The popular team broadcaster and former centerfielder Bobby Murcer died of cancer. Were there any bright spots, any moments of levity? Yes. Ryan Ward was busted by Belmar, New Jersey, police for impersonating Chamberlain. Ward signed autographs for beers and even charged for some of them. But when police saw him tell a bagel shop owner that he was actually Chamberlain, they closed in. The best part of the scam, as long as it lasted? Ward is a Phillies fan who doesn't even like the Yankees.

Nor does a Bronx construction worker and Red Sox fan named Gino Castignoli, who acquired a David Ortiz jersey during construction of the new stadium and buried it in wet concrete — a Curse on the Bambino, one might say. After getting anonymous tips, the Yankees jack hammered out the jersey and presented it to the Jimmy Fund, a pediatric cancer cause associated with the Dana-Farber Institute and the Red Sox. It was auctioned off for $175,100.

At least the season ended on an upswing. In the stadium closer, New York fittingly played Baltimore, birthplace of both the Yankees and Babe Ruth. Munson's son Michael, who was in nursery school when the Yankee catcher died in a 1979 plane crash, stood at home plate in his father's pinstripes and got a slap in the butt from Yogi Berra. When his name was called as a representative of his family, he had to be pushed out to the mound. Afterward, Michael got the old Yankee pitch-

Above: *In 2008, Bobby Abreu proved durable on the bases (22 steals) as well as at the plate (.296 BA, 20 HR, 100 RBI).*

Below: *Joe Girardi in his first year as manager did his best with an injury-riddled team and had to settle for a third-place finish, but in 2009 he led the team to the World Series Championship.*

Above: *In the pre-game ceremony prior to the start of the final game at the old Yankee Stadium on September 21, 2008, manager Joe Girardi (far left) and catcher Jorge Posada (far right) flank old-time Yankees (left to right) David Cone, Don Larsen, Yogi Berra and David Wells.*

Right: *Jose Molina hits what proved to be the last home run at the old Yankee Stadium finale on September 21, 2008.*

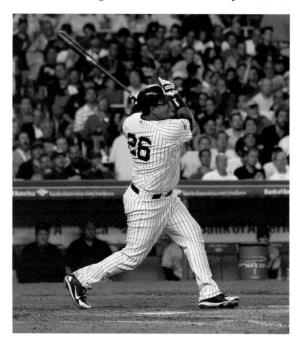

er Ron Guidry to sneak him inside to his old man's locker, still preserved. Michael spoke to his father. His father, he swears, spoke back.

When the game started, the guest commentators on ESPN were Yankee Hall-of-Famers Reggie Jackson, Whitey Ford and Berra. Getting homers from Johnny Damon and Jose Molina to support Pettitte, the Yankees won, 7-3. Molina hit the 83-year-old stadium's last homer, Yankee pinch runner Brett Gardner scored the last run and Rivera got the last out, retiring Brian Roberts. In post-game ceremonies, Jeter thanked fans for their support and told them to "take the memories of this field, add them to the new memories that will come at the new Yankee Stadium and continue to pass them on from generation to generation." Then the Yankees circled the field to the tune of "New York, New York."

There was more bling in the season finale. The starting pitcher was 39-year-old Mike Mussina, who had a 5.15 ERA the previous year. On April 20, 2008, he was 1-3 with a 5.75 ERA and had to read about co-owner Hank Steinbrenner saying he "just needs to learn to pitch like Jamie Moyer," the 45-year-old Phillie. Mussina began "pitching backward," throwing slow stuff while behind on the count. Before long, he had 10 wins and was an All-Star. On the last day of the season, Mussina got a 20-win season for the first time in his career by beating the Red Sox, 6-2, on no runs and three hits over six innings. He appeared to have plenty left in his tank, but he subsequently retired. The first pitcher to win 20 or more in his last season since Sandy Koufax in 1966, Mussina decided to leave on a high note rather than hang on grimly in search of win number 300. Few pitchers win 100 more games than they lose. With a 270-153 record, Mussina has an excellent chance to make the Hall of Fame. He certainly exited as a class act.

Though they won 12 of their last 15 games and enjoyed Mussina's triumph, the Yankees had to deal with missing the play-offs for the first time in a completed season since 1993. They finished in third with an 89-73 record, fully eight games out. But hope will spring eternal when they open the new Yankee Stadium in 2009, next door to the old one. Said Hank Steinbrenner: "There's only so much you can do. They're not supermen. I think it's very simple, we've been devastated by injuries. No team I've ever seen in baseball has been decimated like this. It would kill any team... It's not making excuses. It's reality. That's part of the game. That's clearly our problem. We're going to win it next year. If we need to add a top veteran pitcher, we'll do that." Whereupon the Yankees spent $423.5 million to land prime free agents: left-hander C.C. Sabathia, right-hander A.J. Burnett and first baseman Mark Teixeira.

Left: *Mike Mussina chose to leave baseball in style with his first 20-win season.*

Below: *The new Yankee Stadium as it was nearing completion at the end of 2008. It is adjacent to the site of the old stadium, in the Borough of the Bronx of New York City.*

12. Ascendant, Even Admirable

It wasn't just the $423.5 million the Yankees invested in three free agents, left-hander C.C. Sabathia, right-hander A.J. Burnett and first baseman Mark Teixeira, that had Yankee haters frothing early in 2009. It was the $1.5 billion Yankee Stadium II unveiled in the Bronx.

"With their seats selling for as much as $2,500 a game [later scaled down] while they ask a struggling New York City for an additional $259 million in tax-free bonds to help finance their new stadium and while they sign free agents for well over $400 million—far more than the other 29 major league teams have spent cumulatively—the Yankees present themselves as the very model of arrogance and let-'em-eat-cakeness," Frank Deford declared in an NPR commentary. "Henceforth, I will be calling the Yankees the Antoinettes."

More ridicule followed when the new park was exposed as a wind tunnel that would yield a majors-leading 243 homers. ESPN's Peter Gammons, for one, told the "Mike & Mike" radio audience, "We know that this was not a very well-planned ballpark. Any player that's played there will tell you that it's become one of the biggest jokes in baseball."

Sneering contempt turned to smug satisfaction when onlookers watched the Bronx Bombers struggle out of the gate. Hampered by the two-month absence of third baseman Alex Rodriguez, who in March needed arthroscopic surgery to repair the torn labrum of his right hip, the Yankees went 15-17 through May 12 and lost their first eight games against the archrival Red Sox. It didn't help that A-Rod gave disingenuous answers to questions about his documented use of anabolic steroids while playing the Texas Rangers in 2001-2003. Oh, the *schadenfreude* rocketing around cyberspace!

But after admitting to having used performance enhancing drugs, A-Rod went on to homer May 8 on his first swing of the season, and soon enough the Yankees had the best team in baseball. As the Yankees marched to a baseball-best 103-59 record, eight games ahead of the wild-card Red Sox, Sabathia went 19-8 with a 3.37 ERA, Teixeira led the league with 39 homers and 122 RBI, second baseman Robinson Canó had a breakout .320 season and 39-year-old Mariano Rivera looked positively ageless with 44 saves and .905 walks and hits per nine innings. The most gratifying season of all belonged to shortstop Derek Jeter. Charged with declining skills in the field, he responded by hiring a trainer and made a career-low eight errors in a full season while winning his fourth Gold Glove and leading American League shortstops with a .986 fielding percentage. Jeter batted .334 and had his third 30-steal, 200-hit season, something no other shortstop has done more than once. And he passed Lou Gehrig as alltime Yankee hit leader and Luis Aparicio as career shortstop pacesetter, stretching his total to 2,747 at age 35 and encouraging fantasies of reaching 4,000 or even Pete Rose's record 4,256.

Below: *C.C. Sabathia (left) and A.J. Burnett (right) photographed in the new Yankee Stadium after a press conference announcing their signing on December 18, 2008.*

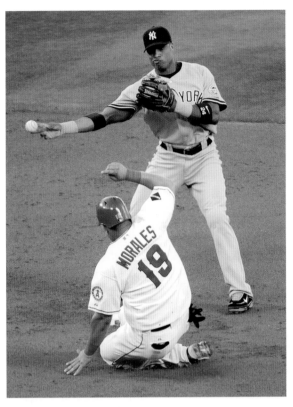

Whatever the dubious merits of Yankee Stadium II, the Yankees feasted there by winning 57 times and set a club record of 237 homers overall. The perfect bookend to the season came from none other than the once injured and despised A-Rod. On the final day, he stood two homers and seven RBI away from 30 and 100 for a record 13th time. When he homered with two on in the sixth, he was one and four short. "I may have one shot," he told teammate Eric Hinske. "We load the bases, I might pop one, you never know." Later that same inning, the Yankees loaded 'em up, and he indeed popped one. In an act of perfect symmetry, A-Rod homered on his first and last swings of the season. His career total of 583 tied Mark McGwire for eighth alltime.

"I think it's fair to say I hit rock bottom this spring, between the embarrassment of the press conference [admitting his substance abuse] and my career being threatened by my hip injury," he told the *New York Times*'s Tyler Kepner. "My life and my career were at a crossroads, and I was either going to stay at the bottom or I was going to bounce back."

The Yankees, for whom excellence is defined by a World Series championship and nothing less, also stood at the crossroads. With the best record in baseball, they could scarcely afford a ninth straight season without a title. The postseason began almost too easily. In the American League Divisional Series, New York beat Minnesota, 7-2, in the opener behind Sabathia's pitching, A-Rod's two run-scoring single and Jeter's crowded box-score line of 2(AB)-3(R)-2(H)-2(RBI)-2(BB). Breaking Twins fans' hearts, the Yankees won Game Two, 4-3, on Teix-

eira's walkoff, 11th-inning homer after A-Rod's earlier game-tying blast. Even though the series shifted west, the Yankees' Andy Pettitte throttled the Twins with a strong 6 2/3 innings and another A-Rod dinger, 4-1, in the clincher. Chipping away at his reputation for postseason choking—he was 0-for-27 with men on base pre-2009—A-Rod batted .455 with two homers and six RBI, while Jeter hit .400.

In the American League Championship Series, the Yankees figured to face a tougher challenge from the Los Angeles Angels of Anaheim, who had just swept the Red Sox. But the Angels never recovered from their jitters in the first two games at Yankee Stadium. First, Sabathia beat them, 4-1, the Yankees getting two runs right off the bat (so to speak) from two singles (one accompanied by outfielder Juan Rivera's throwing error), an A-Rod sacrifice fly, and Hideki Matsui's pop-up that dropped untouched between third baseman Chone Figgins and shortstop Erick Aybar for an RBI single. The Yankees scored another gift run in the sixth when John Lackey's wild pickoff throw advanced Melky Cabrera to second, and he scored when normally sure-handed centerfielder Torii Hunter overran Jeter's single.

An exciting Game Two went five hours, 10 minutes and 13 innings in icy rain before another Angel error proved costly. The Angels took a 3-2 lead in the 11th but Rodriguez, increasingly the go-to guy,

Left: *Robinson Cano, here forcing Kendry Morales of the LA Angels during Game 5 of the 2010 ALCS series, joined the Yankees in 2005 and emerged as a major contributor since 2009.*

Below: *Mark Teixeira celebrates after hitting a walk-off home run in the 11th inning against the Minnesota Twins in Game Two of the ALDS at Yankee Stadium.*

evened it with a leadoff homer in the Yankee half. Then came the 13th. After Jerry Hairston Jr. singled, Brett Gardner sacrificed him to second, Canó was intentionally walked and Cabrera grounded to the left of second baseman Maicer Izturis. Rather than take the sure out at first, Izturis tried for the force at second and threw past Aybar. Backing up the play, Figgins tried to throw home but the ball fell from his grasp and Hairston scored the winning run.

With the Series shifted to Angels Stadium, California won game Three, 5-4, in 11 innings, when Jeff Mathis hit a walkoff double to score Howie Kendrick. Yankee manager Joe Girardi's decision to replace reliever David Robertson with Alfredo Aceves after Robertson had retired the first two batters in the inning backfired and was criticized by the New York media. Since Chien-Ming Wang had been lost for the season after two starts, New York went to an old-fashioned three-man rotation for Game Four. No problem. Working on three days rest, Sabathia and the Yankees won, 10-1, thanks to homers by Johnny Damon and A-Rod Long with Melky Cabrera's four RBI. The Angels bravely staved off elimination in Game Five, scoring three runs after a sixth-run Yankee seventh to win, 7-6. With the bases full of Yankees in the bottom of the ninth, Angels closer Brian Fuentes got Nick Swisher on a game-ending popup.

California fans issued ear-kissing arguments on behalf of the Angels, but Yankee Stadium still spooked them. New York closed out the series in Game Six, 5-2, scoring the final two runs when Kendrick committed a fielding error and pitcher Scott Kashmir

made a throwing error. The redoubtable Rivera recorded a six-out save for Andy Pettitte. For the series, that man C.C. won twice with a 1.12 ERA, and that man A-Rod had three homers, six RBI and a .429 average. It was the Yankees' 40th pennant.

The Fox TV people wanted a Yankee-Dodger World Series for maximum ratings, but they got a more deserving National League entry in the defending champion Philadelphia Phillies. What's more, baseball fans enjoyed the first Fall Classic to go more than five games in six years.

After First Lady Michelle Obama and Second Lady Jill Bidden escorted World War Two veteran and Hall of Farmer Yogi Berra to the plate to receive the first pitch from an Iraq war veteran, the Phillies' Cliff Lee took command of Game One. Yielding just six hits and one unearned run, striking out 10 and walking none, getting two homers from Chase Utley (the first lefty to take Sabathia deep at the Stadium all season), Lee vanquished his old Cleveland Indian teammate and the Yankees, 6-1. A night later, New York's Burnett outpitched a stubborn Pedro Martinez and won Game Two, 3-1. Solo homers by Teixeira and Hideki Matsui gave him all the ballast he needed. For their part, the Phillies were satisfied to have split two at Yankee Stadium.

But when the Series shifted to Philadelphia, you had to search high and low for a home-field advantage. Whittling away the Phillies' early three-run lead, Rodriguez got his first World Series hit, a two-run homer off a TV camera extending over the right-field wall that was originally ruled a ball-in-play double but was later reversed on the Series' inaugural instant replay. The eighth pitcher to drive in a Series run, Pettitte got a game-tying RBI single in the fifth, and the Yankees went on to win it for him, 8-5.

Then New York won a rock-'em, sock-'em Game Four, 7-4, not so much with their big bats as alert baserunning. With two outs in the ninth and the score 4-4, Johnny Damon endured a nine-pitch at bat and singled. Then, with the infield shifting to the right for Teixeira, Damon stole second, noted that third was uncovered by the assigned pitcher or catcher, and kept running for two steals on one pitch. Referencing Enos Slaughter's winning scamper in the 1946 Series, news outlets called this highlight play "Johnny Damon's Mad Dash," and *The New Yorker*'s Roger Angell described it as the "hinge" of the Series. It certainly opened the door. With Damon on third, Philadelphia reliever Brad Lidge delayed throwing his best pitch, a slider that breaks into the dirt and risks rolling to the backstop. Instead, he hit Teixeira with his second pitch, then surrendered the winning run to an ever-resurgent Rodriguez, who doubled to

Below: *Andy Pettite compiled a 54-34 record in his second go-round with the Yankees (2007-2010) and won two games in the 2009 World Series but chose to retire in February 2011.*

left in what he called his career hit. Posada fattened the lead with a two-run single, and Rivera set down the Phils on an eight-pitch ninth. Down three games to one, Philadelphia and Lee outlasted the Yankees, 8-6, in Game Five. Utley's two homers tied Reggie Jackson's record of five in a World Series.

And so another visiting team entered Yankee Stadium needing two wins, with little likelihood of getting them. On November 4, the latest date of any Series game, Pettitte toughed his way through seven innings—an experience that left him on the training table hooked up to an IV drip—and won the clincher, 7-4, getting a Series-tying six RBI from MVP Hideki Matsui. That made Pettitte the first pitcher to win the last game of a divisional series, a league championship series, and a World Series the same year since Boston's Derek Lowe in 2004. Beyond that, Pettitte had now won more (18) postseason games than any pitcher. You want heroes? A-Rod hit .367 in the postseason and Jeter batted .407 against the Phillies. You want unsung heroes? Dámaso Marté, who had a 9:45 ERA in-season, was 0.00 in the postseason and retired the last 12 batters he faced. Matsui, who batted .615, with three homers and eight RBI in the Series, spoke for many Yankees when he admitted, "I guess you could say this is the best moment of my life."

It was the first time the regular-season win leader captured the Series since the 1998 Yankees. With their 27th title, they have won three times as many World Series as the second best team, the Philadelphia/ Kansas City/Oakland A's. Does one dare to say that the 2009 Yankees looked as admirable as they were successful? They used that three-pitcher rotation, the way teams did in the old days. Omitting Pettitte's three-year sabbatical in Houston, stalwarts Pettitte, Posada, Jeter and Rivera have been with the club the last 15 years, like players of yore who spent their entire careers with one team. Nor can you fault the Yankees for improving baseball's best team in 2010. Most notably, they traded outfielder Melky Cabrera to the Braves for righthander Javier Vasquez, a returning Yankee who is one of two pitchers to record 1,000-plus innings with 1,000-plus strikeouts in the last five years and the leader in quality starts (193) over the past decade. That wasn't all. New York let Damon and Matsui go while picking up two less expensive players: Tigers outfielder Curtis Granderson, whose lefthanded stroke is suited for Yankee Stadium's short right-field porch, and first-baseman-DH Nick Johnson, another old Yankee hand, who had a .426 on-base percentage last season at Washington and Florida. Speedy Brett Gardner, who stole 26 bases for the 2009 Yanks, was expected to fill the other depleted outfield spot.

To understand what the latest Yankees acquisitions portend, listen to two *Boston Globe* columnists. Dan Shaughnessy: "Granderson is an All-Star leadoff hitter, a defensive artist in center field, and a 30-home run guy in his prime." Nick Cafardo: "Yankees stole Javier Vasquez."

Look out below!

13. Coming Up Short

In 2010 the Yankees opened and closed their season against the Red Sox for the first time since 1950. New York lost the opener, 9-7, and lost the closer as well, 8-4. A world of events happened in- between.

In a multi-landmark season that seemed to presage good things for the playoffs, the Yankees equaled a franchise record set in 1926 by winning their first five series, and while they were at, it tied their April standard of 12 straight errorless games. On May 8, Mark Teixeira homered three times, the only Yankee other than Babe Ruth and Lou Gehrig to do so. In June, Andy Pettitte won his 200th game as a Yankee, third only to Hall of Famers Whitey Ford (236) and Red Ruffing (231). Jorge Posada had grand slams on consecutive days in June, moving into the select Yankees company of immortals Babe Ruth and Bill Dickey. And on July 2-3 Brett Gardner became the first major leaguer to hit a grand slam one day and an inside-the-park roundtripper the next.

Then came the All-Star break, and with it a multitude of sad news. The longtime Yankee announcer, iconic Bob Sheppard, died on July 11. Two days later, onetime principal owner George Steinbrenner died, followed in another eight days by former New York manager Ralph Houk.

Another Yankee great, the classy manager Joe Torre, and his new team, the Los Angeles Dodgers, played New York, and the Yankees took two of three. By July 18, the Yankees stood at 58-33, their best 91-game mark since 1998. On July 23, Posada drove in his 1,000th run, the 12th Yankee and third catcher after Bill Dickey (1,209) and Yogi Berra (1,430) to do so. Burnishing his Hall of Fame credentials, Posada also became only the fifth catcher in major league history with at least 1,000 RBI, 350 doubles and 250 homers. And on July 25, Robinson Cano got his 1,000th career hit, the fastest homegrown Yankee to that point other than Derek Jeter and Don Mattingly.

Right: *This bronze plaque honors George Steinbrenner, principal owner of the Yankees from 1973 until his death in July 2010. It was installed at Yankee Stadium and dedicated at the start of the 2010 season.*

GEORGE M. STEINBRENNER III
JULY 4, 1930 - JULY 13, 2010

New York Yankees Principal Owner
"The Boss"
1973 - 2010

Purchased the New York Yankees on January 3, 1973.
A true visionary who changed the game of baseball forever,
he was considered the most influential owner in all of sports.
In his 37 years as Principal Owner, the Yankees posted a
Major League-best .566 winning percentage, while winning
11 American League pennants and seven World Series titles,
becoming the most recognizable sports brand in the world.
A devoted sportsman, he was Vice President of the
United States Olympic Committee, a member of the
Baseball Hall of Fame's Board of Directors and a member
of the NCAA Foundation Board of Trustees.
A great philanthropist whose charitable efforts were
mostly performed without fanfare, he followed a personal
motto of the greatest form of charity is anonymity.

Dedicated by the New York Yankees
September 20, 2010

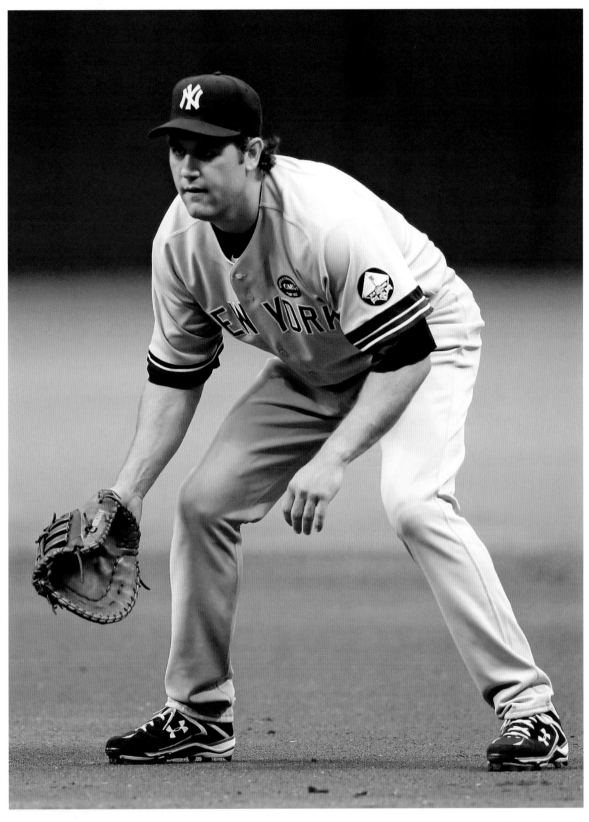

On August 8, Jeter got hit number 2,874 to pass Babe Ruth and assume the Yankee lead, as well as continuing to be the majors' pacesetter among active players. In the same game Alex Rodriguez stole his 300th base to become only the 10th player to get 1,500 runs, 2,500 hits, 200 homers and 300 steals. Of these, only A-Rod, Willie Mays and Barry Bonds have at least 600 homers. And on September 24, Rodriguez hit homers 609 and 610 to move past Sammy Sosa into sixth place on the all-time list.

Four days later the Yankees clinched a playoff spot for the 15th time in the last 16 years. How hard they tried to win the division was a subject of much conjecture. Slipping to 13-17 in September-October after five winning months, they finished second by one game to Tampa Bay at 95-67. Other than losing the home-field advantage, that's no big deal as long as finishing first is only marginally more important than claiming the wild-card spot. Indeed if anything, finishing second was ideal, since it pitted the Yanks in the ALDS against their country cousins from Minnesota, whom they'd vanquished three straight years in postseason series.

The Yankees stormed into Minneapolis with players like Brett Gardner, whose 47 steals were third in the league; Robinson Cano, whose 200 hits were second; Teixeira, whose 113 runs were second to none; and A-Rod, whose 125 RBI placed second. If there was any wrinkle, any spiky little fly in the ointment, it was concern over starting pitching after C.C. Sabathia (league-leading 21 wins), Phil Hughes (18-8) and Andy Pettitte (11-3). Javier Vasquez (10-19, 5.32 ERA, 32 homers allowed), who was left off the postseason roster, and A.J. Burnett (10-15, 5.26 ERA) were dismal failures.

Nonetheless, the Yankees steamed through the ALDS like a Sabathia fastball. The big guy set down the Twins 6-4, in the opener. Trailing 3-0 in the sixth, the Yankees scored four times on run-scoring singles by Cano and Posada, followed by Curtis Granderson's two-run triple. The Twins tied the score in the bottom of the inning, but Teixeira's two-run homer in the seventh gave the Yankees their winning margin. There was a moment of drama in the eighth when the Twins had runners on second and third with two outs. In came Mariano Rivera, inevitable as spring rain, to get Denard Span on a grounder to Jeter.

The following day, Pettitte beat the Twins, 5-2, with Rivera earning another save. Lance Berkman's two-run double settled things, or more accurately unsettled Minnesota manager Ron Gardenhire. Berkman doubled home another run in the seventh after the Twins thought

they had him struck out on a 1-2 pitch, and Gardenhire argued so vehemently he got the heave-ho from umpire Hunter Wendelstedt.

Back in New York, the Yankees swept the series with Hughes and four relievers setting down the Twins 6-1. Two more Yankee heroes, Nick Swisher and Marcus Thames, homered.

In the American League Championship Series, the Yankees faced the Texas Rangers, who had never played in a World Series or done much else in their 39-year history. But these were not your father's Rangers. Team president Nolan Ryan had thrown out pitch counts as a measure of pitcher fatigue, giving his starters added confidence, and no batting order that included the league's Most Valuable Player, Josh Hamilton, could be ignored.

Game One looked auspicious for Rangers starter C.J. Wilson, who was cruising along with a 5-1 lead when the floodgates opened in the eighth inning. Gardner reached first on an infield single, and Jeter doubled the speedster home. Rangers manager Ron Washington replaced Wilson with Darren Oliver, who promptly walked Swisher and Teixeira to load the bases. Darren O'Day replaced Oliver and gave up a two-run single to Rodriguez, cutting the lead to 5-4. With Clay Rapada in for O'Day, Cano singled Teixeira home: 5-5. Derek Holland came in, and Thames singled to center, scoring Rodriguez and giving the Yankees a 6-5 lead. Naturally Rivera preserved the win.

Above: *Nick Swisher, here hitting a solo home run in Game 5 of the 2010 AL Championship series against the Rangers, joined the Yankees in 2009 and, if lacking spectacular stats, has been a consistent and competent addition to the team.*

So was the Rangers' Achilles heel their bullpen? Not so fast. In Game Two Colby Lewis beat the Yankees 7-2, but 3 1/3 innings of one hit relief — this time from Rapada, Alexi Ogando, Oliver, O'Day and Neftali Feliz, respectively — made the difference. Then Cliff Lee stunned a crowd of 49,480 at Yankee Stadium II with eight innings of 13-strikeout, two-hit ball to win Game Three, 8-0. The Yankees reached Tommy Hunter for three runs in 3 1/3 innings to lead Game Four, 3-2, but Holland sped through 3 2/3 innings without allowing a run while the Rangers kayoed Burnett and won, 10-3. Little noted at the time but long remembered afterward, Teixeira left the game — and the series — after pulling his left hamstring while running to first in the fifth inning.

Behind Sabathia the Yankees won Game Five, 7-2, but that just delayed the inevitable. Lee promptly finished them off 6-2 in Game Six, and the Rangers won the series four games to two.

Which brings us back to the Teixeira injury in Game Four. Writing in Bleacher Report, Doug Rush argued that "it was as if [he was] representing the Yankees in the series, having one of their legs go out from underneath and playing short-handed."

It was just as well that George Steinbrenner didn't live long enough to

see such an up-and-down season. It would have killed him.

To scour the Internet during the 2011 season was to discover endless explanations of why the Yankees wouldn't survive the postseason, if they even got that far: the failure to sign top free agents; the mighty Red Sox and Phillies; A-Rod's injuries. Indeed, news initially focused more on individuals than team performance, and not always positively.

Early in the season, catcher-DH Jorge Posada asked out of the lineup on the day when he was slated to bat ninth for the first time in his career. He later apologized and made significant contributions, but the bloom was off his rose. Attention quickly switched to Derek Jeter, whose winter salary dispute had cast him and G.M. Brian Cashman in unflattering light. Jeter began the season 64 hits short of 3,000. Slumping early and getting extra-base hits about as often as we see Halley's Comet, Jeter was disabled in June with a torn calf muscle. During his 21-day absence, the team went 14-4, and critics wondered if Jeter should be dropped from his leadoff position when he returned.

Back in the lineup and with two hits to go on July 9, Jeter blossomed. He went 5-for-5, homered for #3,000, stole a base and drove in the go-ahead run when the

Above: *Derek Jeter here hits one for the record books on July 9, 2011--a homerun for his 3,000th hit as a Yankee. What many fans at first were surprised to hear is that no previous Yankee—including--Babe Ruth and Joe DiMaggio—had ever reached this goal.*

Yankees beat the Rays 5-4. The staggering performance reminded us of Jeter's career brilliance. The 28th player and the fourth youngest to reach 3,000, he is the only one to make it in a Yankee uniform. No one else — not Ruth, Gehrig, DiMaggio, Berra, Jackson, Winfield or Mattingly — reached the milestone with the club.

Alas, 48 hours later, July 11, 2011, loomed as a day in Yankee history that would live in infamy. Alex Rodriguez had arthroscopic surgery for a torn meniscus in his right knee, and might as well have been lost for the season because he batted under .200 after his return. It was his second surgery in three years. "Boy, aren't they glad they signed him for six more years," Mike Lupica of the New York Daily News said on ESPN's "Sports Reporters." Later there was also a brief brouhaha over Major League Baseball investigating Rodriguez for playing in illegal poker games. Big deal!

Meanwhile, Roger Clemens, who had pitched for the Yankees (1999-2003, 2007), was undermining his legacy. On the same July 11, he went on trial for perjury and obstruction of Congress relating to his 2008 testimony in which he denied using illegal performance-enhancing drugs. Three days later, Judge Reggie Walton declared a mistrial. Incredibly, the prosecution had permitted previously disallowed hearsay evidence--Andy Pettitte's wife Laura

Right: *Righthander David Robertson joined the Yankees in 2008 and has become a reliable reliever, appearing in over 60 innings in 2010 and 2011.*

saying in an affidavit that Andy told her Roger admitted illegal drug use to him--to be heard by the jury. "The most shocking, inexplicable error in modern baseball history has taken place in a courtroom, not on a field," Thomas Boswell wrote in the Washington Post.

By the end of the month the defense asked for a dismissal of charges on the grounds that, curiouser and curiouser, the prosecution had deliberately sabotaged its case because it was going badly. If Clemens was at least temporarily spared a guilty verdict and possible jail term, he was not given a pass by the media or the public. Most knowledgeable observers had to conclude he'd used illegal drugs and would never be admitted to the Hall of Fame.

Did anyone notice that a season was progressing? Actually, a fine one. The little-noted addition of veterans Freddy Garcia and Bartolo Colon solidified a rotation including CC Sabathia, spectacular (16-4, 3.70 ERA) rookie Ivan Nova, and the much-maligned A.J. Burnett for the first-half season. Manager Joe Girardi's deft touch with his generally subpar staff-- smoother than his waspish behavior toward games rescheduled after Hurricane Irene--helped the underdog Yankees climb to first place in the second half of the season. Centerfielder Curtis Granderson put up MVP-quality numbers (41 homers, 119 RBI, .916 OPS), ably abetting a latter-day Murderers Row that featured Mark Teixeira and linchpin Robinson Cano and didn't even need A-Rod's contribution.

If there was any doubt that fans were watching an offensive juggernaut, the Yankees became the first team to hit three grand slams in a single game when Cano, catcher Russell Martin and Granderson connected on August 25.

If there was any doubt the Yankees possessed a superlative lefthander, it was erased on July 10 when the Yankees and Rays staged the rarest of games in today's climate of pitch-count fealty and foreshortened starts: a bona fide pitcher's duel. Nineteen-game winner Sabathia and the Rays' James Shields went the distance in a symphonic 1-0 New York victory. "In the top of the ninth, with one out to go for the win, the fans were on their feet, shouting, coaxing, trying to will Sabathia, still on the mound, to get that final strike," New York Times music critic Anthony Tommasini wrote. "The shouts of encouragement had a little bit of 'don't you dare blow it' mixed in. Imagine opera buffs standing up and shouting before a tenor's climactic high C. "Sabathia did the job, the fans screamed, and the baseball symphony concluded, though broke up is the more precise musical term, since the chatter continued as people filed out of the exits."

Finally, if there was any doubt the Yankees had the greatest reliever of all time, Mariano Rivera erased it by recording an all-time MLB record 602nd save on September 19. He was, moreover,

Below: *Brett Gardner joined the Yankees and as a leftfielder has had four solid seasons. His BA (.264) has not been anything special but he has had a solid on-base % (.353) and slugging % (.368) and in 2011 stole 49 bases.*

Above: *Curtis Granderson is "high-fived" by Mark Teixeira after his homerun in April against Toronto, one of his 41 homers in 2011. Joining the Yankees in 2010, Granderson had his career-best season in 2011.*

getting astonishing set-up work from David Robertson, who allowed eight runs in 70 outings.

It all added up to a 97-65 record — the league's best — and an AL East title. Not that the Yankees had a free ride to the World Series. In the best-of-five divisional playoffs, they faced Detroit's Cy Young Award winner Justin Verlander, who was prepared to go in Game One and Game Five if needed. Then luck intervened. On September 30, Game One was suspended by rain after 1 ½ innings with Sabathia and Verlander in a 1-1 duel. That meant Verlander could be used for a full start only in Game Three.

When Game One resumed on October 1, Nova replaced Sabathia, allowed two runs on four hits in 6 1/3 innings and outdueled Verlander's successor, Doug Fister, 9-3. Max Scherzer threw 5 1/3 innings of hitless ball against Garcia, and Detroit won Game Two, 5-3, when closer Jose Valverde retired Cano with two men on in the ninth. The Tigers added a Game Three win when the 28-year-old Verlander showed better recuperative powers on two days' rest than 31-year-old Sabathia, struck out 11 Yankees and beat Sabathia, 5-4, with another Valverde save. Facing possible elimination, the Yankees got 5 2/3 innings of one-run ball from Burnett and two circus catches saving four runs by Granderson to spark a 10-1 win in Game Four.

In the win-or-go-home Game Five, a rematch between Nova and Fister in Yankee Stadium, first-inning homers by Austin Jackson and Don Kelly gave the Tigers a 2-0 lead and quieted the home crowd. Murmurs turned to moans when Nova left after two innings with a flexor strain in his forearm, and Girardi began running in relievers like a fire brigade. Phil Hughes pitched a scoreless 1 1/3 innings and Boone Logan two-thirds of an inning before Girardi turned to Sabathia, who had never relieved in the majors. After Jackson doubled to left, Kelly and Delmon Young struck out. Sabathia gave Miguel Cabrera an intentional walk, when Girardi elected to face Victor Martinez instead. Bad move! Martinez singled to score Jackson and give the Tigers a 3-0 lead.

Meanwhile, Fister pitched five strong innings, working out of a bases-loaded situation in the fourth and finally yielding a Cano homer in the fifth to make it 3-1. Then Detroit manager Jim Leyland turned to his bullpen but declined the use Verlander. Another moonlighting starter, Scherzer, pitched 1 1/3 innings before giving way to setup man Joaquin Benoit with one out and a man on in the seventh. Benoit gave the Yankees every opportunity when Granderson singled and Cano reached on an infield hit Benoit might have fielded, loading the bases. Whereupon A-Rod struck out, Benoit walked Teixeira to force in a run and Steve Swisher fanned. That made it 3-2, but the Yankees could get no closer than Jeter's long fly with Brett Gardner on in the eighth. Another Valverde save, another season prematurely over.

Their Game Five starter wasn't New York's only nova. Assessing the playoff performance of the 4-5-6 hitters, the New York Post called A-Rod (.111 average, 0 homers, 3 RBI), Teixeira (.167, 0, 1) and Swisher (.211, 1, 1) "The Three Stooges." Polled by the Daily News, readers overwhelmingly voted to dump Rodriguez. But was all this anger justified? Anything can happen in a short series, and baseball may be the toughest sport to predict results in (see Phillies, Red Sox). The trouble with the Yankees is, they set the bar unnecessarily high. "We are the Yankees," team president Randy Levine, channeling Douglas MacArthur's "no substitute for victory," told ESPN. "When you don't win the World Series, it is a bitter disappointment and not a successful year."

A challenge for the 2011 Yankees!

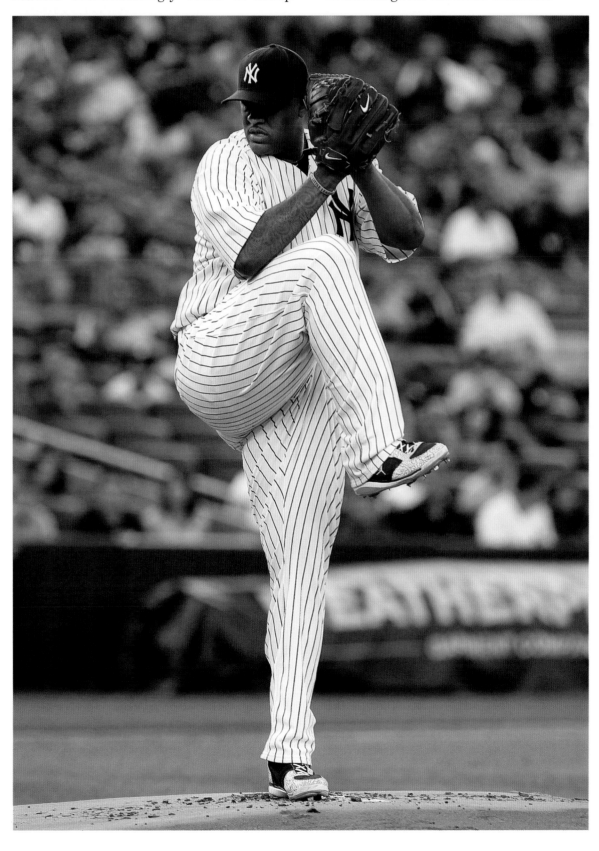

Left: *C.C. Sabathia, the Yankees ace lefthander, joined the team in 2009 with what was then the highest pitcher's salary in MLB history. Although he lost his one appearance in the 2009 World Series, his three strong seasons (19-8, 21-7, and 19-8) have helped to get the Yankees into postseason play.*

Yankee Achievements

YEAR-BY-YEAR YANKEES STANDINGS

Year	Pos.	Record	Games Behind	Manager	Year	Pos.	Record	Games Behind	Manager
1903	4	72-62	17	Griffith	1957	1	98-56	+8	Stengel
1904	2	92-59	1½	Griffith	1958	1	92-62	+10	Stengel
1905	6	71-78	21½	Griffith	1959	3	79-75	15	Stengel
1906	2	90-61	3	Griffith	1960	1	97-57	+8	Stengel
1907	5	70-78	21	Griffith	1961	1	109-53	+8	Houk
1908	8	51-103	39½	Griffith/ Elberfeld	1962	1	96-66	+5	Houk
1909	5	74-77	23½	Griffith	1963	11	104-57	+10½	Houk
1910	2	88-63	14½	Stallings/Chase	1964	1	99-63	+1	Berra
1911	6	76-76	25½	Chase	1965	6	77-85	25	Keane
1912	8	50-102	55	Wolverton	1966	10	70-89	26½	Keane/Houk
1913	7	57-94	38	Chance	1967	9	72-90	20	Houk
1914	6	70-84	30	Chance/ Peckingpaugh	1968	5	83-79	20	Houk
1915	5	69-83	32½	Donovan	1969	5	80-81	28½	Houk
1916	4	80-74	11	Donovan	1970	2	93-69	15	Houk
1917	6	71-82	28½	Donovan	1971	4	82-80	21	Houk
1918	4	60-63	13½	Huggins	1972	4	79-76	6½	Houk
1919	3	80-59	7½	Huggins	1973	4	80-82	17	Houk
1920	3	95-59	3	Huggins	1974	2	89-73	2	Virdon
1921	1	98-55	+4½	Huggins	1975	3	83-77	12	Virdon/Martin
1922	1	94-60	+1	Huggins	1976	1	97-62	+10½	Martin
1923	1	98-54	+16	Huggins	1977	1	100-62	+2½	Martin
1924	2	89-63	2	Huggins	1978	1	100-63	+1	Martin/Lemon
1925	7	69-85	30	Huggins	1979	4	89-71	13½	Lemon/Martin
1926	1	91-63	+3	Huggins	1980	1	103-59	+3	Howser
1927	1	110-44	+19	Huggins	1981	¼	59-48	x	Michael/Lemon
1928	1	101-53	+2½	Huggins	1982	5	79-83	16	Lemon/Michael/ King
1929	2	88-66	18	Huggins/ Fletcher	1983	3	91-71	7	Martin
1930	3	86-68	16	Shawkey	1984	3	87-75	17	Berra
1931	2	94-59	13½	McCarthy	1985	2	97-64	2	Berra/Martin
1932	1	107-47	+13	McCarthy	1986	2	90-72	5½	Piniella
1933	2	91-59	7	McCarthy	1987	4	89-73	9	Piniella
1934	2	94-60	7	McCarthy	1988	5	85-76	3½	Martin/Piniella
1935	2	89-60	3	McCarthy	1989	5	74-87	14½	Greene/Dent
1936	1	102-51	+19½	McCarthy	1990	7	67-95	21	Dent/Merrill
1937	1	102-52	+13	McCarthy	1991	5	71-91	20	Merrill
1938	1	99-53	+9½	McCarthy	1992	4	76-86	20	Showalter
1939	1	106-45	+17	McCarthy	1993	2	88-74	7	Showalter
1940	3	88-66	2	McCarthy	1994	1	70-43	+6½y	Showalter
1941	1	101-53	+17	McCarthy	1995	2	79-65	7z	Showalter
1942	1	103-51	+9	McCarthy	1996	1	92-70	+4	Torre
1943	1	98-56	+13½	McCarthy	1997	2	96-66	2z	Torre
1944	3	83-71	6	McCarthy	1998	1	114-48	+22	Torre
1945	4	81-71	6½	McCarthy	1999	1	98-64	+4	Torre
1946	3	87-67	17	McCarthy/ Dickey/Neun	2000	1	87-74	+2½	Torre
1947	1	97-57	+12	Harris	2001	1	95-65	+13½	Torre
1948	3	94-60	2½	Harris	2002	1	103-58	+10½	Torre
1949	1	97-57	+1	Stengel	2003	1	101-61	+6	Torre
1950	1	98-56	+3	Stengel	2004	1	101-61	+3	Torre
1951	1	98-56	+5	Stengel	2005	1	95-67	0a	Torre
1952	1	95-59	+2	Stengel	2006	1	97-65	+10	Torre
1953	1	99-52	+8½	Stengel	2007	2	98-86	2z	Torre
1954	2	103-51	8	Stengel	2008	3	89-73	8	Girardi
1955	1	96-58	+3	Stengel	2009	1	103-59	0	Girardi
1956	1	97-57	+9	Stengel	2010	2	95-67	2	Girardi
					2011	1	97-65	+6	Girardi

x = split season
y = strike year; no post-season play
z = won AL wild-card
a = awarded division title; won tiebreaker by defeating Red Sox in season series

SINGLE-SEASON YANKEE BATTING RECORDS

Category	Player	Value	Year
Batting Average (500 ABs)	Babe Ruth	.393	1923
Hits	Don Mattingly	238	1986
Home Runs	Roger Maris	61	1961
Runs Batted In	Lou Gehrig	184	1931
Singles	Steve Sax	171	1989
Doubles	Don Mattingly	53	1986
Triples	Earle Combs	23	1927
Slugging Percentage	Babe Ruth	.847	1920
Strikeouts	Alfonso Soriano	157	2002
Hitting Streak	Joe DiMaggio	56	1941
Grand Slam Home Runs	Don Mattingly	6	1987

SINGLE-SEASON YANKEE PITCHING RECORDS

Category	Player	Value	Year
Wins	Jack Chesbro	41	1904
Losses	Joe Lake	22	1908
ERA (150 Innings)	Spud Chandler	1.64	1943
Winning percentage	Tom Zachary	1.000	1929
(10 Decisions)	Aaron Small	1.000	2005
Strikeouts	Ron Guidry	248	1978
Saves	Mariano Rivera	53	2004
Innings Pitched	Jack Chesbro	454	1904
Game Appearances	Paul Quantrill	86	2004
Shutouts	Ron Guidry	9	1978
No-Hitters	Allie Reynolds	2	1951

YANKEES POST-SEASON RECORD
Playoffs

Year	Opponent	Win-Loss
1976	Kansas City Royals	3-2
1977	Kansas City Royals	3-2
1978	Boston Red Sox	
	(division playoff)	1-0
	Kansas City Royals	3-1
1980	Kansas City Royals	0-3
1981	ALDS – Milwaukee Brewers	3-2
	ALCS – Oakland Athletics	3-0
1995	ALDS – Seattle Mariners	2-3
1996	ALDS – Texas Rangers	3-1
	ALCS – Baltimore Orioles	4-1
1997	ALDS – Cleveland Indians	2-3
1998	ALDS – Texas Rangers	3-0
	ALCS – Cleveland Indians	4-2
1999	ALDS – Texas Rangers	3-0
	ALCS – Boston Red Sox	4-1
2000	ALDS – Oakland Athletics	3-2
	ALCS – Seattle Mariners	4-2
2001	ALDS – Oakland Athletics	3-2
	ALCS – Seattle Mariners	4-1
2002	ALDS – Anaheim Angels	1-3
2003	ALDS – Minnesota Twins	3-1
	ALCS – Boston Red Sox	4-3
2004	ALDS – Minnesota Twins	3-1
	ALCS – Boston Red Sox	3-4
2005	ALDS – Los Angeles Angels	1-3
2006	ALDS – Detroit Tigers	1-3
2007	ALDS – Cleveland Indians	1-3
2009	ALDS – Minnesota Twins	3-0
	ALCS – Los Angeles Angels	4-2
2010	ALDS – Minnesota Twins	3-0
	ALCS – Texas Rangers	2-4
2011	ALDS – Detroit Tigers	2-3

ALDS = American League Division Series
ALCS = American League Championship Series

World Series

Year	Opponent	Win-Loss
1921	New York Giants	3-5
1922	New York Giants	0-4-1
1923	New York Giants	4-2
1926	St. Louis Cardinals	3-4
1927	Pittsburgh Pirates	4-0
1928	St. Louis Cardinals	4-0
1932	Chicago Cubs	4-0
1936	New York Giants	4-2
1937	New York Giants	4-1
1938	Chicago Cubs	4-0
1939	Cincinnati Reds	4-0
1941	Brooklyn Dodgers	4-1
1942	St. Louis Cardinals	1-4
1943	St. Louis Cardinals	4-1
1947	Brooklyn Dodgers	4-3
1949	Brooklyn Dodgers	4-1
1950	Philadelphia Phillies	4-0
1951	New York Giants	4-2
1952	Brooklyn Dodgers	4-3
1953	Brooklyn Dodgers	4-2
1955	Brooklyn Dodgers	3-4
1956	Brooklyn Dodgers	4-3
1957	Milwaukee Braves	3-4
1958	Milwaukee Braves	4-3
1960	Pittsburgh Pirates	3-4
1961	Cincinnati Reds	4-1
1962	San Francisco Giants	4-3
1963	Los Angeles Dodgers	0-4
1964	St. Louis Cardinals	3-4
1976	Cincinnati Reds	0-4
1977	Los Angeles Dodgers	4-2
1978	Los Angeles Dodgers	4-2
1981	Los Angeles Dodgers	2-4
1996	Atlanta Braves	4-2
1998	San Diego Padres	4-0
1999	Atlanta Braves	4-0
2000	New York Mets	4-1
2001	Arizona Diamondbacks	3-4
2003	Florida Marlins	2-4
2009	Philadelphia Phillies	4-2

ALL-TIME YANKEE CAREER BATTING LEADERS

Games Played	Derek Jeter	2426
At Bats	Derek Jeter	9868
Hits	Derek Jeter	3088
Batting Average	Babe Ruth	.349
Home Runs	Babe Ruth	659
Runs Scored	Babe Ruth	1959
Runs Batted In	Lou Gehrig	1991
Strikeouts	Mickey Mantle	1710
Stolen Bases	Rickey Henderson	326

ALL-TIME YANKEE CAREER PITCHING LEADERS

Innings Pitched	Whitey Ford	3171
Wins	Whitey Ford	236
Losses	Mel Stottlemyre	139
Winning Percentage (100 decisions)	Spud Chandler	.717
ERA (800 inn.)	Mariano Rivera	2.21
Strikeouts	Whitey Ford	1956
Game Appearances	Mariano Rivera	1042
Shutouts	Whitey Ford	45
No-Hitters	Allie Reynolds	2
Perfect Game	Don Larsen, 1956 World Series	
	David Wells, 1998	
	David Cone, 1999	
Saves	Mariano Rivera	603

HALL OF FAMERS

Name	Position	Year Elected
Babe Ruth	OF	1936
Lou Gehrig	1B	1939
Willie Keeler	OF	1939
Clark Griffith	P, Manager	1945
Frank Chance	1B, Manager	1946
Jack Chesbro	P	1946
Herb Pennock	P	1948
Paul Waner	OF	1952
Ed Barrow	Executive	1953
Bill Dickey	C	1954
Frank Baker	3B	1955
Joe DiMaggio	OF	1955
Dazzy Vance	P	1955
Joe McCarthy	Manager	1957
Bill McKechnie	3B	1962
Burleigh Grimes	P	1964
Miller Huggins	Manager	1964
Casey Stengel	Manager	1966
Red Ruffing	P	1967
Stan Coveleski	P	1969
Waite Hoyt	P	1969
Earle Combs	OF	1970
George Weiss	Executive	1971
Yogi Berra	C, OF, Manager	1972
Lefty Gomez	P	1972
Mickey Mantle	OF, 1B	1974
Whitey Ford	P	1974
Bucky Harris	Manager	1975
Bob Lemon	Manager	1976
Joe Sewell	3B	1977
Larry MacPhail	Executive	1978
Johnny Mize	1B, PH	1981
Enos Slaughter	OF, PH	1985
Catfish Hunter	P	1987
Tony Lazzeri	2B/3B	1991
Gaylord Perry	P	1991
Reggie Jackson	OF/DH	1993
Leo Durocher	SS/2B	1994
Phil Rizzuto	SS	1994
Phil Niekro	P	1997
Lee MacPhail	Executive	1998
Dave Winfield	OF	2001
Wade Boggs	3B	2005
Rich "Goose" Gossage	P	2008
Joe Gordon	2B	2009

Index